Professional Exam

Paper C03

FUNDAMENTALS OF BUSINESS MATHEMATICS

CIMA EXAM PRACTICE KIT

PAPER C03 : FUNDAMENTALS OF BUSINESS MATHEMATICS

Published by: Kaplan Publishing UK

Unit 2 The Business Centre, Molly Millars Lane, Wokingham, Berkshire RG41 2QZ

Copyright © 2013 Kaplan Financial Limited. All rights reserved.

No part of this publication may be reproduced, stored in a retrieval system or transmitted in any form or by any means electronic, mechanical, photocopying, recording or otherwise without the prior written permission of the publisher.

Acknowledgements

We are grateful to the CIMA for permission to reproduce past examination questions. The answers to CIMA Exams have been prepared by Kaplan Publishing, except in the case of the CIMA November 2010 and subsequent CIMA Exam answers where the official CIMA answers have been reproduced.

Notice

The text in this material and any others made available by any Kaplan Group company does not amount to advice on a particular matter and should not be taken as such. No reliance should be placed on the content as the basis for any investment or other decision or in connection with any advice given to third parties. Please consult your appropriate professional adviser as necessary. Kaplan Publishing Limited and all other Kaplan group companies expressly disclaim all liability to any person in respect of any losses or other claims, whether direct, indirect, incidental, consequential or otherwise arising in relation to the use of such materials.

British Library Cataloguing in Publication Data

A catalogue record for this book is available from the British Library

ISBN: 978-0-85732-964-6

Printed and bound in Great Britain.

CONTENTS

	Page
Syllabus Guidance, Learning Objectives and Verbs	vii
Examination Techniques	xv
Mathematical Tables	xvii

Section

1	Practice questions	1
2	Objective test questions	23
3	Answers to practice questions	53
4	Answers to objective test questions	87
5	Mock Assessment 1	109
6	Mock Assessment 2	121
7	Answers to Mock Assessment 1	133
8	Answers to Mock Assessment 2	141

PAPER C03 : FUNDAMENTALS OF BUSINESS MATHEMATICS

INDEX TO QUESTIONS AND ANSWERS

PAGE NUMBER

PRACTICE QUESTIONS

	QUESTION	ANSWER
BASIC MATHEMATICS	1	53
FORMULAE	1	53
PERCENTAGES, RATIOS AND PROPORTIONS	3	55
ACCURACY AND ROUNDING	4	56
EQUATIONS AND GRAPHS	5	57
PROBABILITY	6	59
PROBABILITY THEORY	6	59
EXPECTED VALUE AND DECISION-MAKING	8	61
SUMMARISING AND ANALYSING DATA	10	64
PRESENTATION OF DATA	10	64
AVERAGES	12	67
VARIATION	13	70
THE NORMAL DISTRIBUTION	14	72
INTERRELATIONSHIP BETWEEN VARIABLES	15	74
CORRELATION AND REGRESSION	15	74
FORECASTING	17	77
TIME SERIES	17	77
FINANCIAL MATHEMATICS	18	79
SPREADSHEETS	19	82

OBJECTIVE TEST QUESTIONS

BASIC MATHEMATICS	23	87
FORMULAE	23	87
PERCENTAGES, RATIOS AND PROPORTIONS	25	88
ACCURACY AND ROUNDING	27	90
EQUATIONS AND GRAPHS	27	90
PROBABILITY	30	94
PROBABILITY THEORY	30	94
EXPECTED VALUE AND DECISION-MAKING	32	95

PAPER C03 : FUNDAMENTALS OF BUSINESS MATHEMATICS

PAGE NUMBER

	QUESTION	*ANSWER*
SUMMARISING AND ANALYSING DATA	34	97
PRESENTATION OF DATA	34	97
AVERAGES	36	98
VARIATION	38	99
THE NORMAL DISTRIBUTION	39	100
INDEX NUMBERS	40	102
INTERRELATIONSHIP BETWEEN VARIABLES	42	103
CORRELATION AND REGRESSION	42	103
FORECASTING	44	104
TIME SERIES	44	104
FINANCIAL MATHEMATICS	45	105
SPREADSHEETS	47	106

SYLLABUS GUIDANCE, LEARNING OBJECTIVES AND VERBS

A THE CERTIFICATE IN BUSINESS ACCOUNTING

The Certificate introduces you to management accounting and gives you the basics of accounting and business. There are five subject areas, which are all tested by computer-based assessment (CBA). The five papers are:

- Fundamentals of Management Accounting
- Fundamentals of Financial Accounting
- Fundamentals of Business Mathematics
- Fundamentals of Business Economics
- Fundamentals of Ethics, Corporate Governance and Business Law

The Certificate is both a qualification in its own right and an entry route to the next stage in CIMA's examination structure.

The examination structure after the Certificate comprises:

- Managerial Level
- Strategic Level
- Test of Professional Competence (an exam based on a case study).

B AIMS OF THE SYLLABUS

The aims of the syllabus are:

- to provide for the Institute, together with the practical experience requirements, an adequate basis for assuring society that those admitted to membership are competent to act as management accountants for entities, whether in manufacturing, commercial or service organisations, in the public or private sectors of the economy;

- to enable the Institute to examine whether prospective members have an adequate knowledge, understanding and mastery of the stated body of knowledge and skills;

- to complement the Institute's practical experience and skills development requirements.

C STUDY WEIGHTINGS

A percentage weighting is shown against each topic in the syllabus. This is intended as a guide to the proportion of study time each topic requires.

All topics in the syllabus must be studied, since any single examination question may examine more than one topic, or carry a higher proportion of marks than the percentage study time suggested.

The weightings *do not* specify the number of marks that will be allocated to topics in the examination.

PAPER C03 : FUNDAMENTALS OF BUSINESS MATHEMATICS

D LEARNING OUTCOMES

Each topic within the syllabus contains a list of learning outcomes, which should be read in conjunction with the knowledge content for the syllabus. A learning outcome has two main purposes:

1. to define the skill or ability that a well-prepared candidate should be able to exhibit in the examination;

2. to demonstrate the approach likely to be taken by examiners in examination questions.

The learning outcomes are part of a hierarchy of learning objectives. The verbs used at the beginning of each learning outcome relate to a specific learning objective, for example, evaluate alternative approaches to budgeting.

The verb 'evaluate' indicates a high level learning objective. As learning objectives are hierarchical, it is expected that at this level, students will have knowledge of different budgeting systems and methodologies and be able to apply them.

A list of the learning objectives and the verbs that appear in the syllabus learning outcomes and examinations, follows:

Learning objectives	Verbs used	Definition
1 Knowledge		
What you are expected to know	List	Make a list of
	State	Express, fully or clearly, the details of/facts of
	Define	Give the exact meaning of
2 Comprehension		
What you are expected to understand	Describe	Communicate the key features of
	Distinguish	Highlight the differences between
	Explain	Make clear or intelligible/State the meaning of
	Identify	Recognise, establish or select after consideration
	Illustrate	Use an example to describe or explain something
3 Application		
How you are expected to apply your knowledge	Apply	To put to practical use
	Calculate/compute	To ascertain or reckon mathematically
	Demonstrate	To prove with certainty or to exhibit by practical means
	Prepare	To make or get ready for use
	Reconcile	To make or prove consistent/compatible
	Solve	Find an answer to
	Tabulate	Arrange in a table

SYLLABUS GUIDANCE, LEARNING OBJECTIVES AND VERBS

4 Analysis

How you are expected to analyse the detail of what you have learned

Analyse	Examine in detail the structure of
Categorise	Place into a defined class or division
Compare and contrast	Show the similarities and/or differences between
Construct	To build up or compile
Discuss	To examine in detail by argument
Interpret	To translate into intelligible or familiar terms
Produce	To create or bring into existence

5 Evaluation

How you are expected to use your learning to evaluate, make decisions or recommendations

Evaluation

Advise	To counsel, inform or notify
Evaluate	To appraise or assess the value of
Recommend	To advise on a course of action

E COMPUTER-BASED ASSESSMENT

CIMA has introduced computer-based assessment (CBA) for all subjects at Certificate level. CIMA uses objective test questions in the computer-based assessment. The most common types are:

- multiple choice, where you have to choose the correct answer from a list of four possible answers. This could either be numbers or text.
- multiple choice with more choices and answers – for example, choosing two correct answers from a list of eight possible answers. This could either be numbers or text.
- single numeric entry, where you give your numeric answer e.g. profit is $10,000.
- multiple entry, where you give several numeric answers e.g. the charge for electricity is $2000 and the accrual is $200.
- true/false questions, where you state whether a statement is true or false e.g. external auditors report to the directors is FALSE.
- matching pairs of text e.g. the convention 'prudence' would be matched with the statement' inventories revalued at the lower of cost and net realisable value'.
- other types could be matching text with graphs and labelling graphs/diagrams.

In this Exam Practice Kit we have used these types of questions.

For further CBA practice, CIMA Publishing has produced CIMA eSuccess CD-ROMs for all certificate level subjects. These will be available from www.cimapublishing.com

F FUNDAMENTALS OF BUSINESS MATHEMATICS

The assessment for Fundamentals of Business Mathematics is a two hour computer-based assessment comprising 45 compulsory questions, with one or more parts. Single part questions are generally worth 1–2 marks each, but two and three part questions may be worth 4 or 6 marks. There will be no choice and all questions should be attempted if time permits. CIMA are continuously developing the question styles within the CBA system and you are advised to try the on-line website demo at www.cimaglobal.com/cba, to both gain familiarity with assessment software and examine the latest style of questions being used.

G SYLLABUS OUTLINE

Syllabus overview

This paper primarily deals with the tools and techniques to understand the mathematics associated with managing business operations. Probability and risk play an important role in developing business strategy. Preparing forecasts and establishing the relationships between variables are an integral part of budgeting and planning.

Financial mathematics provides an introduction to interest rates and annuities and to investment appraisal for projects. Preparing graphs and tables in summarised formats and using spreadsheets are important in both the calculation of data and the presentation of information to users.

Syllabus structure

The syllabus comprises the following topics and study weightings:

A	Basic mathematics	15%
B	Probability	15%
C	Summarising and analysing data	15%
D	Relationships between variables	15%
E	Forecasting	15%
F	Financial mathematics	15%
G	Spreadsheets	10%

Assessment strategy

There will be a two hour computer based assessment, comprising 45 compulsory questions, each with one or more parts.

A variety of objective test question styles and types will be used within the assessment.

SYLLABUS GUIDANCE, LEARNING OBJECTIVES AND VERBS

C03 – A. BASIC MATHEMATICS (15%)

Learning outcomes
On completion of their studies students should be able to:

Lead	Component	Level	Indicative syllabus content
1. demonstrate the use of basic mathematics.	(a) calculate answers using formulae; (b) calculate percentages and proportions; (c) calculate answers to appropriate decimal places or significant figures.	3 3 3	• Use of formulae, including negative powers as in the formula for the learning curve. [1] • Order of operations in formulae, including brackets, powers and roots. [1] • Percentages and ratios. [1] • Rounding of numbers. [1]
2. solve equations and inequalities.	(a) solve simple equations, including two variable simultaneous equations and quadratic equations; (b) prepare graphs of linear and quadratic equations; (c) solve simple inequalities.	3 3 3	• Basic algebraic techniques and solution of equations, including simultaneous equations and quadratic equations. [1] • Graphs of linear and quadratic equations. [1] • Manipulation of inequalities. [1]

C03 – B. PROBABILITY (15%)

Learning outcomes
On completion of their studies students should be able to:

Lead	Component	Level	Indicative syllabus content
1. calculate probability.	(a) calculate simple probability; (b) demonstrate the addition and multiplication rules of probability; (c) calculate a simple conditional probability.	3 3 3	• Probability and its relationship with proportion and percent. [8] • Addition and multiplication rules of probability theory. [8] • Venn diagrams. [8]
2. demonstrate the use of probability where risk and uncertainty exists.	(a) calculate an expected value; (b) demonstrate the use of expected value tables in decision making; (c) explain the limitations of expected values; (d) explain the concepts of risk and uncertainty.	3 3 2 2	• Expected values and expected value tables. [8] • Risk and uncertainty. [8]

PAPER C03 : FUNDAMENTALS OF BUSINESS MATHEMATICS

C03 – C. SUMMARISING AND ANALYSING DATA (15%)

Learning outcomes
On completion of their studies students should be able to:

Lead	Component	Level	Indicative syllabus content
1. apply techniques for summarising data.	(a) explain the difference between data and information; [2]	2	• Data and information. [2] • Tabulation of data. [2] • Graphs, charts and diagrams: scatter diagrams, histograms, bar charts and ogives. [2] • Summary measures of central tendency and dispersion for both grouped and ungrouped data. [3] • Frequency distributions. [3] • Normal distribution. [8]
	(b) identify the characteristics of good information; [2]	2	
	(c) tabulate data; [2]	3	
	(d) prepare graphs, charts and diagrams; [2]	3	
	(e) calculate for both ungrouped and grouped data. arithmetic mean, median, mode, range, variance, standard deviation and coefficient of variation; [3]	3	
	(f) explain the concept of frequency distribution; [2]	2	
	(g) prepare graphs/diagrams of normal distribution; [3]	3	
	(h) explain the properties of normal distribution; [8]	2	
	(i) demonstrate the use of normal distribution tables. [8]	3	
2. apply techniques for analysing data.	(a) apply the Pareto distribution and the '80:20' rule; [3]	3	• Pareto distribution and the '80:20 rule'. [3] • Index numbers. [4]
	(b) explain how and why indices are used; [4]	2	
	(c) calculate indices using either base or current weights; [4]	3	
	(d) apply indices to deflate a series. [4]	3	

C03 – D. RELATIONSHIPS BETWEEN VARIABLES (15%)

Learning outcomes
On completion of their studies students should be able to:

Lead	Component	Level	Indicative syllabus content
1. calculate correlation coefficient for bivariate data.	(a) prepare a scatter diagram;	3	• Scatter diagrams. [5] • Correlation coefficient: Spearman's rank correlation coefficient and Pearson's correlation coefficient. [5]
	(b) calculate the correlation coefficient and the coefficient of determination between two variables.	3	
2. apply techniques of simple regression.	(e) calculate the regression equation between two variables;	3	• Simple linear regression. [5]
	(f) apply the regression equation to predict the dependent variable, given a value of the independent variable.	3	

C03 – E. FORECASTING (15%)

Learning outcomes
On completion of their studies students should be able to:

Lead	Component	Level	Indicative syllabus content
1. demonstrate techniques used for forecasting.	(a) prepare a time series graph;	3	• Time series analysis – graphical analysis. [6] • Trends in time series – graphs, moving averages and linear regressions. [6]
	(b) identify trends and patterns using an appropriate moving average;	2	
	(c) identify the components of a time series model;	2	
	(d) prepare a trend equation using either graphical means or regression analysis.	3	
2. prepare forecasts.	(a) calculate seasonal factors for both additive and multiplicative models;	3	• Seasonal variations using both additive and multiplicative models. [6] • Forecasting and its limitations. [6]
	(b) explain when each of the additive or multiplicative models is appropriate;	2	
	(c) calculate predicted values given a time series model;	3	
	(d) identify the limitations of forecasting models.	2	

C03 – F. FINANCIAL MATHEMATICS (15%)

Learning outcomes
On completion of their studies students should be able to:

Lead	Component	Level	Indicative syllabus content
1. calculate present and future values of cash flows.	(a) calculate future values of an investment using both simple and compound interest;	3	• Simple and compound interest. [7] • Present value (including using formulae and CIMA tables). [7] • Annuities and perpetuities. [7]
	(b) calculate an annual percentage rate of interest given a monthly or quarterly rate;	3	
	(c) calculate the present value of a future cash sum;	3	
	(d) calculate the present value of an annuity and a perpetuity.	3	
2. apply financial mathematical techniques.	(a) calculate loan/mortgage repayments and the value of the loan/mortgage outstanding;	3	• Loans and mortgages. [7] • Sinking funds and savings funds (including using formulae for the sum of a geometric progression). [7] • Discounting to find net present value (NPV) and internal rate of return (IRR). [7] • The concept of shareholder value. [7] • Interpretation of NPV and IRR. [7]
	(b) calculate the future value of regular savings and/or the regular investment needed to generate a required future sum;	3	
	(c) calculate the net present value (NPV) and the internal rate of return (IRR) of a project;	3	
	(d) explain whether and why a project should be accepted or rejected.	2	

PAPER C03 : FUNDAMENTALS OF BUSINESS MATHEMATICS

C03 – G. SPREADSHEETS (10%)

Learning outcomes
On completion of their studies students should be able to:

Lead	Component	Level	Indicative syllabus content
1. apply spreadsheets to calculate and present data.	(a) explain the features and functions of spreadsheet software;	2	• Features and functions of commonly used spreadsheet software: workbook, worksheet, rows, columns, cells, data, text, formulae, formatting, printing, graphics and macros. [9]
	(b) explain the use and limitations of spreadsheet software in business;	2	***Note:*** knowledge of Microsoft Excel type spreadsheet vocabulary/formulae syntax is required. Formulae tested will be that which is constructed by users rather than pre-programmed formulae. [9]
	(c) apply spreadsheet software to the normal work of a Chartered Management Accountant.	3	• Advantages and disadvantages of spreadsheet software, when compared to manual analysis and other types of software application packages. [9]
• Use of spreadsheet software in the day-to-day work of the Chartered Management Accountant: budgeting, forecasting, reporting performance, variance analysis, what-if analysis, discounted cash flow calculations. [9]

EXAMINATION TECHNIQUES

COMPUTER-BASED EXAMINATIONS

TEN GOLDEN RULES

1. Make sure you are familiar with the software before you start exam. You cannot speak to the invigilator once you have started.

2. These exam practice kits give you plenty of exam style questions to practise.

3. Attempt all questions, there is no negative marking.

4. Double check your answer before you put in the final answer.

5. On multiple choice questions (MCQs), there is only one correct answer.

6. Not all questions will be MCQs – you may have to fill in missing words or figures.

7. Identify the easy questions first and get some points on the board to build up your confidence.

8. Try and allow 15 minutes at the end to check your answers and make any corrections.

9. If you don't know the answer, try a process of elimination.

10. Work out your answer on paper first if it is easier for you. Scrap paper will be provided for you. You are allowed to take pens, pencils and rulers with you to the examination, but you are not allowed pencil cases, phones, paper or notes, or a calculator.

GUIDANCE RE CIMA ONLINE CALCULATOR

As part of the CIMA Certificate level computer based assessment software, candidates are now provided with a calculator. This calculator is onscreen and is available for the duration of the assessment. The calculator is available in each of the five Certificate level assessments and is accessed by clicking the calculator button in the top left hand corner of the screen at any time during the assessment.

All candidates must complete a 15 minute tutorial before the assessment begins and will have the opportunity to familiarise themselves with the calculator and practice using it.

Candidates may practise using the calculator by downloading and installing the practice exam at http://www.vue.com/athena/ The calculator can be accessed from the fourth sample question (of 12).

Please note that the practice exam and tutorial provided by Pearson VUE at http://www.vue.com/athena/ is not specific to CIMA and includes the full range of question types the Pearson VUE software supports, some of which CIMA does not currently use.

MATHEMATICAL TABLES

PROBABILITY

A ∪ B = A or B. A ∩ B = A and B (overlap).

P(B \ A) = probability of B, given A.

Rules of Addition

If A and B are mutually exclusive: P(A ∪ B) = P(A) + P(B)

If A and B are **not** mutually exclusive: P(A ∪ B) = P(A) + P(B) − P(A ∩ B)

Rules of Multiplication

If A and B are *independent*: P(A ∩ B) = P(A) * P(B)

If A and B are **not** *independent*: P(A ∩ B) = P(A) * P(B \ A)

E(X) = expected value = probability * payoff

Quadratic Equations

If $aX^2 + bX + c = 0$ is the general quadratic equation, the two solutions (roots) are given by:

$$X = \frac{-b \pm \sqrt{b^2 - 4ac}}{2a}$$

DESCRIPTIVE STATISTICS

Arithmetic Mean $\bar{x} = \frac{\Sigma x}{n}$ $\bar{x} = \frac{\Sigma fx}{\Sigma f}$ (frequency distribution)

Standard Deviation $SD = \sqrt{\frac{\Sigma(x - \bar{x})^2}{n}}$ $SD = \sqrt{\frac{\Sigma fx^2}{\Sigma f} - \bar{x}^2}$ (frequency distribution)

INDEX NUMBERS

Price relative = 100 P_1/P_0 Quantity relative = 100 Q_1/Q_0

Price: Σ W * P_1/P_0 W * 100, where W denotes weights

Quantity: Σ W *; Q_1/Q_0/Σ W * 100, where W denotes weights

TIME SERIES

Additive Model   Series = Trend + Seasonal + Random

Multiplicative Model   Series = Trend * Seasonal * Random

PAPER C03 : FUNDAMENTALS OF BUSINESS MATHEMATICS

LINEAR REGRESSION AND CORRELATION

The linear regression equation of Y on X is given by:

$$Y = a + bX \text{ or } Y - \bar{Y} = b(X - \bar{X})$$

where

$$b = \frac{\text{Covariance (XY)}}{\text{Variance (X)}} = \frac{n\Sigma XY - (\Sigma X)(\Sigma Y)}{n\Sigma X^2 - (\Sigma X)^2}$$

and

$$a = \bar{Y} - b\bar{X}$$

or solve

$$\Sigma Y = na + b\Sigma X$$
$$\Sigma XY = a\Sigma X + b\Sigma X^2$$

Coefficient of correlation

$$r = \frac{\text{Covariance (XY)}}{\sqrt{\text{Var(X).Var(Y)}}} = \frac{n\Sigma XY - (\Sigma X)(\Sigma Y)}{\sqrt{\{n\Sigma X^2 - (\Sigma X)^2\}\{n\Sigma Y^2 - (\Sigma Y)^2\}}}$$

$$R(\text{rank}) = 1 - \frac{6\Sigma d^2}{n(n^2 - 1)}$$

FINANCIAL MATHEMATICS

Compound Interest (Values and Sums)

Future Value S, of a sum of X, invested for n periods, compounded at $r\%$ interest

$$S = X[1 + r]^n$$

Annuity

Present value of an annuity of £1 per annum receivable or payable for n years, commencing in one year, discounted at $r\%$ per annum:

$$PV = \frac{1}{r}\left[1 - \frac{1}{[1+r]^n}\right]$$

Perpetuity

Present value of £1 per annum, payable or receivable in perpetuity, commencing in one year, discounted at $r\%$ per annum:

$$PV = \frac{1}{r}$$

Note: Logarithm tables are also available when you sit for your assessment.

AREA UNDER THE NORMAL CURVE

This table gives the area under the normal curve between the mean and a point Z standard deviations above the mean. The corresponding area for deviations below the mean can be found by symmetry.

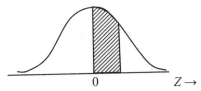

$Z = \frac{(x-\mu)}{\partial}$	0.00	0.01	0.02	0.03	0.04	0.05	0.06	0.07	0.08	0.09
0.0	.0000	.0040	.0080	.0120	.0159	.0199	.0239	.0279	.0319	.0359
0.1	.0398	.0438	.0478	.0517	.0557	.0596	.0636	.0675	.0714	.0753
0.2	.0793	.0832	.0871	.0910	.0948	.0987	.1026	.1064	.1103	.1141
0.3	.1179	.1217	.1255	.1293	.1331	.1368	.1406	.1443	.1480	.1517
0.4	.1554	.1591	.1628	.1664	.1700	.1736	.1772	.1808	.1844	.1879
0.5	.1915	.1950	.1985	.2019	.2054	.2088	.2123	.2157	.2190	.2224
0.6	.2257	.2291	.2324	.2357	.2389	.2422	.2454	.2486	.2518	.2549
0.7	.2580	.2580	.2611	.2642	.2673	.2704	.2734	.2794	.2823	.2852
0.8	.2881	.2910	.2939	.2967	.2995	.3023	.3051	.3078	.3106	.3133
0.9	.3159	.3186	.3212	.3238	.3264	.3289	.3315	.3340	.3365	.3389
1.0	.3413	.3438	.3461	.3485	.3508	.3531	.3554	.3577	.3599	.3621
1.1	.3643	.3665	.3686	.3708	.3729	.3749	.3770	.3790	.3810	.3830
1.2	.3849	.3869	.3888	.3907	.3925	.3944	.3962	.3980	.3997	.4015
1.3	.4032	.4049	.4066	.4082	.4099	.4115	.4131	.4147	.4162	.4177
1.4	.4192	.4207	.4222	.4236	.4251	.4265	.4279	.4292	.4306	.4319
1.5	.4332	.4345	.4357	.4370	.4382	.4394	.4406	.4418	.4430	.4441
1.6	.4452	.4463	.4474	.4485	.4495	.4505	.4515	.4525	.4535	.4545
1.7	.4554	.4564	.4573	.4582	.4591	.4599	.4608	.4616	.4625	.4633
1.8	.4641	.4649	.4656	.4664	.4671	.4678	.4686	.4693	.4699	.4706
1.9	.4713	.4719	.4726	.4732	.4738	.4744	.4750	.4756	.4762	.4767
2.0	.4772	.4778	.4783	.4788	.4793	.4798	.4803	.4808	.4812	.4817
2.1	.4821	.4826	.4830	.4834	.4838	.4842	.4846	.4850	.4854	.4857
2.2	.4861	.4865	.4868	.4871	.4875	.4878	.4881	.4884	.4887	.4890
2.3	.4893	.4896	.4898	.4901	.4904	.4906	.4909	.4911	.4913	.4916
2.4	.4918	.4920	.4922	.4925	.4927	.4929	.4931	.4932	.4934	.4936
2.5	.4938	.4940	.4941	.4943	.4945	.4946	.4948	.4949	.4951	.4952
2.6	.4953	.4955	.4946	.4957	.4959	.4960	.4961	.4962	.4963	.4964
2.7	.4965	.4966	.4967	.4968	.4969	.4970	.4971	.4972	.4973	.4974
2.8	.4974	.4975	.4977	.4977	.4978	.4979	.4979	.4980	.4980	.4981
2.9	.4981	.4982	.4983	.4983	.4984	.4984	.4985	.4985	.4986	.4986
3.0	**.49865**	.4987	.4987	.4988	.4988	.4989	.4989	.4989	.4990	.4990
3.1	**.49903**	.4991	.4991	.4991	.4992	.4992	.4992	.4992	.4993	.4993
3.2	**.49931**	.4993	.4994	.4994	.4994	.4994	.4994	.4995	.4995	.4995
3.3	**.49952**	.4995	.4995	.4996	.4996	.4996	.4996	.4996	.4996	.4997
3.4	**.49966**	.4997	.4997	.4997	.4997	.4997	.4997	.4997	.4997	.4998
3.5	**.49977**									

PRESENT VALUE TABLE

Present value of $1, that is $(1+r)^{-n}$ where r = interest rate; n = number of periods until payment or receipt.

Periods (n)	Interest rates (r)									
	1%	2%	3%	4%	5%	6%	7%	8%	9%	10%
1	0.990	0.980	0.971	0.962	0.952	0.943	0.935	0.926	0.917	0.909
2	0.980	0.961	0.943	0.925	0.907	0.890	0.873	0.857	0.842	0.826
3	0.971	0.942	0.915	0.889	0.864	0.840	0.816	0.794	0.772	0.751
4	0.961	0.924	0.888	0.855	0.823	0.792	0.763	0.735	0.708	0.683
5	0.951	0.906	0.863	0.822	0.784	0.747	0.713	0.681	0.650	0.621
6	0.942	0.888	0.837	0.790	0.746	0.705	0.666	0.630	0.596	0.564
7	0.933	0.871	0.813	0.760	0.711	0.665	0.623	0.583	0.547	0.513
8	0.923	0.853	0.789	0.731	0.677	0.627	0.582	0.540	0.502	0.467
9	0.914	0.837	0.766	0.703	0.645	0.592	0.544	0.500	0.460	0.424
10	0.905	0.820	0.744	0.676	0.614	0.558	0.508	0.463	0.422	0.386
11	0.896	0.804	0.722	0.650	0.585	0.527	0.475	0.429	0.388	0.350
12	0.887	0.788	0.701	0.625	0.557	0.497	0.444	0.397	0.356	0.319
13	0.879	0.773	0.681	0.601	0.530	0.469	0.415	0.368	0.326	0.290
14	0.870	0.758	0.661	0.577	0.505	0.442	0.388	0.340	0.299	0.263
15	0.861	0.743	0.642	0.555	0.481	0.417	0.362	0.315	0.275	0.239
16	0.853	0.728	0.623	0.534	0.458	0.394	0.339	0.292	0.252	0.218
17	0.844	0.714	0.605	0.513	0.436	0.371	0.317	0.270	0.231	0.198
18	0.836	0.700	0.587	0.494	0.416	0.350	0.296	0.250	0.212	0.180
19	0.828	0.686	0.570	0.475	0.396	0.331	0.277	0.232	0.194	0.164
20	0.820	0.673	0.554	0.456	0.377	0.312	0.258	0.215	0.178	0.149

Periods (n)	Interest rates (r)									
	11%	12%	13%	14%	15%	16%	17%	18%	19%	20%
1	0.901	0.893	0.885	0.877	0.870	0.862	0.855	0.847	0.840	0.833
2	0.812	0.797	0.783	0.769	0.756	0.743	0.731	0.718	0.706	0.694
3	0.731	0.712	0.693	0.675	0.658	0.641	0.624	0.609	0.593	0.579
4	0.659	0.636	0.613	0.592	0.572	0.552	0.534	0.516	0.499	0.482
5	0.593	0.567	0.543	0.519	0.497	0.476	0.456	0.437	0.419	0.402
6	0.535	0.507	0.480	0.456	0.432	0.410	0.390	0.370	0.352	0.335
7	0.482	0.452	0.425	0.400	0.376	0.354	0.333	0.314	0.296	0.279
8	0.434	0.404	0.376	0.351	0.327	0.305	0.285	0.266	0.249	0.233
9	0.391	0.361	0.333	0.308	0.284	0.263	0.243	0.225	0.209	0.194
10	0.352	0.322	0.295	0.270	0.247	0.227	0.208	0.191	0.176	0.162
11	0.317	0.287	0.261	0.237	0.215	0.195	0.178	0.162	0.148	0.135
12	0.286	0.257	0.231	0.208	0.187	0.168	0.152	0.137	0.124	0.112
13	0.258	0.229	0.204	0.182	0.163	0.145	0.130	0.116	0.104	0.093
14	0.232	0.205	0.181	0.160	0.141	0.125	0.111	0.099	0.088	0.078
15	0.209	0.183	0.160	0.140	0.123	0.108	0.095	0.084	0.079	0.065
16	0.188	0.163	0.141	0.123	0.107	0.093	0.081	0.071	0.062	0.054
17	0.170	0.146	0.125	0.108	0.093	0.080	0.069	0.060	0.052	0.045
18	0.153	0.130	0.111	0.095	0.081	0.069	0.059	0.051	0.044	0.038
19	0.138	0.116	0.098	0.083	0.070	0.060	0.051	0.043	0.037	0.031
20	0.124	0.104	0.087	0.073	0.061	0.051	0.043	0.037	0.031	0.026

MATHEMATICAL TABLES

Cumulative present value of $1 per annum, Receivable or Payable at the end of each year for n years $\frac{1-(1+r)^{-n}}{r}$

Periods (n)	Interest rates (r)									
	1%	2%	3%	4%	5%	6%	7%	8%	9%	10%
1	0.990	0.980	0.971	0.962	0.952	0.943	0.935	0.926	0.917	0.909
2	1.970	1.942	1.913	1.886	1.859	1.833	1.808	1.783	1.759	1.736
3	2.941	2.884	2.829	2.775	2.723	2.673	2.624	2.577	2.531	2.487
4	3.902	3.808	3.717	3.630	3.546	3.465	3.387	3.312	3.240	3.170
5	4.853	4.713	4.580	4.452	4.329	4.212	4.100	3.993	3.890	3.791
6	5.795	5.601	5.417	5.242	5.076	4.917	4.767	4.623	4.486	4.355
7	6.728	6.472	6.230	6.002	5.786	5.582	5.389	5.206	5.033	4.868
8	7.652	7.325	7.020	6.733	6.463	6.210	5.971	5.747	5.535	5.335
9	8.566	8.162	7.786	7.435	7.108	6.802	6.515	6.247	5.995	5.759
10	9.471	8.983	8.530	8.111	7.722	7.360	7.024	6.710	6.418	6.145
11	10.368	9.787	9.253	8.760	8.306	7.887	7.499	7.139	6.805	6.495
12	11.255	10.575	9.954	9.385	8.863	8.384	7.943	7.536	7.161	6.814
13	12.134	11.348	10.635	9.986	9.394	8.853	8.358	7.904	7.487	7.103
14	13.004	12.106	11.296	10.563	9.899	9.295	8.745	8.244	7.786	7.367
15	13.865	12.849	11.938	11.118	10.380	9.712	9.108	8.559	8.061	7.606
16	14.718	13.578	12.561	11.652	10.838	10.106	9.447	8.851	8.313	7.824
17	15.562	14.292	13.166	12.166	11.274	10.477	9.763	9.122	8.544	8.022
18	16.398	14.992	13.754	12.659	11.690	10.828	10.059	9.372	8.756	8.201
19	17.226	15.679	14.324	13.134	12.085	11.158	10.336	9.604	8.950	8.365
20	18.046	16.351	14.878	13.590	12.462	11.470	10.594	9.818	9.129	8.514

Periods (n)	Interest rates (r)									
	11%	12%	13%	14%	15%	16%	17%	18%	19%	20%
1	0.901	0.893	0.885	0.877	0.870	0.862	0.855	0.847	0.840	0.833
2	1.713	1.690	1.668	1.647	1.626	1.605	1.585	1.566	1.547	1.528
3	2.444	2.402	2.361	2.322	2.283	2.246	2.210	2.174	2.140	2.106
4	3.102	3.037	2.974	2.914	2.855	2.798	2.743	2.690	2.639	2.589
5	3.696	3.605	3.517	3.433	3.352	3.274	3.199	3.127	3.058	2.991
6	4.231	4.111	3.998	3.889	3.784	3.685	3.589	3.498	3.410	3.326
7	4.712	4.564	4.423	4.288	4.160	4.039	3.922	3.812	3.706	3.605
8	5.146	4.968	4.799	4.639	4.487	4.344	4.207	4.078	3.954	3.837
9	5.537	5.328	5.132	4.946	4.772	4.607	4.451	4.303	4.163	4.031
10	5.889	5.650	5.426	5.216	5.019	4.833	4.659	4.494	4.339	4.192
11	6.207	5.938	5.687	5.453	5.234	5.029	4.836	4.656	4.486	4.327
12	6.492	6.194	5.918	5.660	5.421	5.197	4.988	7.793	4.611	4.439
13	6.750	6.424	6.122	5.842	5.583	5.342	5.118	4.910	4.715	4.533
14	6.982	6.628	6.302	6.002	5.724	5.468	5.229	5.008	4.802	4.611
15	7.191	6.811	6.462	6.142	5.847	5.575	5.324	5.092	4.876	4.675
16	7.379	6.974	6.604	6.265	5.954	5.668	5.405	5.162	4.938	4.730
17	7.549	7.120	6.729	6.373	6.047	5.749	5.475	5.222	4.990	4.775
18	7.702	7.250	6.840	6.467	6.128	5.818	5.534	5.273	5.033	4.812
19	7.839	7.366	6.938	6.550	6.198	5.877	5.584	5.316	5.070	4.843
20	7.963	7.469	7.025	6.623	6.259	5.929	5.628	5.353	5.101	4.870

Section 1

PRACTICE QUESTIONS

BASIC MATHEMATICS

FORMULAE

1 Simplify the following expressions

    (i) $5a + 6b + 2a - 3b$

    (ii) $4x + 3x - 2x - x$

    (iii) $3b + 4c - 2b + 5c$

    (iv) $2a + 3x - 4y + 2a + 2y - 3x$

    (v) $3x + 9y - 4x + 5y - 2z$

2 Expand the following expressions

    (i) $5(2x + 3y - 4z)$

    (ii) $-x(2 + 3x)$

    (iii) $-4(x - 2y + 3z)$

    (iv) $3x(2x - 4y + 3z)$

    (v) $-4y(2y + 4y - 3z)$

3 Simplify the following expressions

    (i) $2a^2 \times a^3$

    (ii) $3a^2 \times 2a^3$

    (iii) $3x^3 \times 12x^4$

    (iv) $(3a^2b)^3$

    (v) $(2a^2x)^2$ when $a = 2$ and $x = 3$

PAPER C03 : FUNDAMENTALS OF BUSINESS MATHEMATICS

4 Simplify the following expressions

(i) $x^5 \div x^2$

(ii) $x^9 \div x^7$

(iii) $15x^5 \div 3x^4$

(iv) $a^6 \div a^6$

(v) $a^5 \div a^7$

5 Calculate the following values

(i) $3^{0.5}$

(ii) $2^{0.5}$

(iii) $4^{1.5}$

(iv) 10^{-3}

(v) $36^{-0.5}$

6 Calculate

(i) $\dfrac{3}{4} + \dfrac{2}{5}$

(ii) $\dfrac{7}{8} - \dfrac{3}{16}$

(iii) $\dfrac{1}{3} \times \dfrac{1}{5}$

(iv) $\dfrac{3}{4} \div \dfrac{2}{5}$

(v) $1\tfrac{5}{7} + 3\tfrac{2}{3}$

7 In the formula $Q = \sqrt{\dfrac{2DC}{PR}}$ If C = 10, P = 6, R = 0.2, D = 600

What is the value of Q?

8 In the formula $Q = \sqrt{\dfrac{2CD}{H}}$ If C = $20, D = 24,000, H = $6

What is the value of Q?

PRACTICE QUESTIONS : SECTION 1

9 State whether the following statements are true or false.

(i) It does not matter in which order multiplications are carried out if there are brackets shown.

(ii) The top of a fraction is called the denominator,

(iii) The bottom of a fraction is called the numerator.

(iv) When two or more powers of the same number are multiplied, the individual indices must be added.

(v) The decimal fraction of a log number is called the mantissa.

(vi) The whole number of a log is called the characteristic

(vii) The cube root of 64 is 4.

(viii) A negative index is calculated by taking the inverse of the number.

(ix) 15/8 is a larger number than 1.75.

(x) The numerical value of $\dfrac{(x^3)^3}{x^7}$ when x = 5 is 25

PERCENTAGES, RATIOS AND PROPORTIONS

10 If VAT is levied on goods and services at 17½%, how much VAT is paid on goods costing VAT inclusive?

(i) $117.50

(ii) $150

(iii) $200

(iv) $250

(v) $500

11 Equipment is sold for $240 and the cost price is $200. Calculate

(i) the gross profit.

(ii) the profit mark up.

12 If sales are $500 and gross profit is $200, express the gross profit as

(i) a fraction

(ii) a decimal

(iii) a percentage

(iv) a ratio

PAPER C03 : FUNDAMENTALS OF BUSINESS MATHEMATICS

13 James, Fred and Martin are in a business partnership and over the past year have made a profit of $50,000. They have agreed to split profit in the ratio of 5:7:8. How much profit is awarded to

  (i)   James

  (ii) Fred

  (iii) Martin

14 Three balls (red, white and blue) are put into a bag. How many different ways are there of pulling the balls out?

15 Company Y offers its customers a 12% discount on all orders over $500 and 15% on all orders over $1,000. If customer A spends $1,200 and customer B $650, how much discount do they end up giving away?

16 State whether the following statements are true or false.

  (i)   To convert a fraction into a % multiply by 100.

  (ii) A proportion cannot be measured as a decimal.

  (iii) If 8 dogs are picked for the final of a dog show, and 3 are to be picked 1st, 2nd and 3rd, There are 500 possible results.

  (iv) A person pays $228 for goods having received a discount of 5%. The undiscounted price was $250.

  (v)   x% of 300 = 3x

  (vi) An article is sold for $300 VAT inclusive. The vendor receives $300 which is credited to sales.

ACCURACY AND ROUNDING

17 Complete the following phrase or sentence.

  (i)   A .... variable is one that can assume any value.

  (ii) A .... variable is one that can only assume certain values.

  (iii) An .... variable is one which is not affected by changes in another.

  (iv) A .... variable is affected by changes in another.

  (v)   When individuals are rounded in the same direction, this is a .... error.

  (vi) When individuals are rounded in either direction this is an .... error.

18 Calculate 32.6 + 4.32 and the error if the figures have been rounded to three significant figures.

19 Calculate 32.6 − 4.32 and the error if the figures have been rounded to three significant figures.

PRACTICE QUESTIONS : SECTION 1

20 Calculate 32.6 × 4.32 and the error if the figures have been rounded to three significant figures.

21 A product priced at $56.99 has been reduced to $52.49. To two decimal places, the percentage reduction in price is?

EQUATIONS AND GRAPHS

22 Solve the following equations

(i) $3x + 4y = 25$ $\qquad$ $4x + 5y = 32$

(ii) $x + y = 10$ $\qquad$ $x - 4y = 0$

(iii) $2x + 3y = 42$ $\qquad$ $5x - y = 20$

(iv) $\dfrac{x}{3} + \dfrac{y}{2} = 7$ $\qquad$ $\dfrac{2x}{3} - \dfrac{y}{6} = 7$

23 Simultaneous equations. Solve the following

(i) $2x + 3y + 4z = 9$ $\qquad$ (1)

(ii) $3x - 2y - 3z = 3$ $\qquad$ (2)

(iii) $4x + 5y - 2z = 25$ $\qquad$ (3)

24 Factorise the following expressions

(i) $am + bm + an + bn$

(ii) $12a^2m^3 - 15am^5$

(iii) $x^2 + 4x - 12$

(iv) $10p^2 + 11pq - 6q^2$

(v) $3x^2 + 6x$

25 Quadratic equations. Solve the following

(i) $9x^2 - 30x + 25 = 0$

(ii) $3x^2 - 20x + 15 = 40$

(iii) $x^2 + 6x + 9 = 25$

26 Solve the following by factorisation if possible, otherwise use the formula.

(i) $x^2 - 5x + 6 = 0$

(ii) $x^2 + 6x + 7 = 0$

(iii) $x^2 - 6x + 9 = 0$

(iv) $2x^2 - 5x + 20 = 0$

27 State whether the following statements are true or false?
   (i)   In the equation y = a + bx, y is the dependant variable.
   (ii)   The shape of a linear demand curve is a straight line,
   (iii) Quadratic equations can never be solved by factorisation,
   (iv)   If $(b^2 - 4ac)$ is zero, there is only one solution to the equation.
   (v)   If $(b^2 - 4ac)$ is positive, there are no real solutions,
   (vi)   If x + y = 9 then both x and y must be positive.
   (vii) The formula used to solve quadratic equations is $x = \dfrac{-b \pm \sqrt{(b^2 - 4ac)}}{2a}$
   (viii) Quadratic equations cannot be solved by using a graph.

PROBABILITY

PROBABILITY THEORY

28 If a card is pulled out of a pack of playing cards at random what is the probability that it is
   (i)   black
   (ii)   a club
   (iii) an ace
   (iv)   the ace of spades

29 Fill in the missing word
   (i)   Where the probability of an event is calculated by a process of logical reasoning, this is known as ………………… probability.
   (ii)   When a situation can be repeated a number of times this is classed as ………………… probability.
   (iii) Where estimates are made by individuals of the relative likelihood of events occurring, this is called ………………… probability.
   (iv)   A pictorial representation in which terms of a mathematical statement are shown by overlapping circles is known as a ………………… diagram.

30 City and United play each other twice per season. Each side has an equal chance of winning in a match between them. Frank Green, a local bookmaker, publishes odds of either of the teams to win both games at 5-1. Is Frank expected to lose money with these odds?

PRACTICE QUESTIONS : SECTION 1

31 There are 500 fish in a lake. There are 200 pike, 150 perch, 100 trout and 50 salmon. Each fish has an equal chance of being caught.

(i) What is the probability that a pike is caught first?

(ii) What is the probability that a pike or a perch is caught first?

(iii) What is the probability that a pike, perch or salmon is caught first?

(iv) What is the probability that a perch is not caught first?

(v) What is the probability that neither a salmon nor a trout is caught first?

32 In a room there are 100 CIMA students. Fifty per cent are male and 50% are female. Sixty per cent are fully qualified, 40% are partly qualified. What is the probability of selecting at random a student who is

(i) male?

(ii) fully qualified?

(iii) male and qualified?

(iv) male or qualified?

(v) female and qualified?

33 Twenty-five per cent of new cars of a particular model are supplied from factory X. The remainder come from factory Y. Ten per cent of factory X's output has a major fault whilst 18% of factory Y's output has the same fault.

(i) What is the probability that a car selected at random has a major defect?

(ii) What is the probability it was made at factory X?

(iii) What is the probability it was made at factory Y?

34 A box contains four red balls, two white balls and a yellow ball. If three balls are selected at random and there is no replacement between each selection what is the probability of selecting

(i) three of the same colour?

(ii) one of each colour?

35 If we toss a fair coin two times

(i) what is the probability that first toss is a head?

(ii) what is the probability that both tosses will be heads?

(iii) what is the probability that neither tosses will be heads?

(iv) what is the probability that a head would not appear in three consecutive tosses?

PAPER C03 : FUNDAMENTALS OF BUSINESS MATHEMATICS

36 A travel agent keeps a stock of holiday brochures. Currently there is a total of 500 brochures in stock, as follows: 285 for European holidays, 90 for American holidays, 110 for Asian holidays and 15 for African holidays. A brochure is selected at random.

Calculate the following probabilities

(i) that a European brochure is selected

(ii) that an African brochure is NOT selected

(iii) that neither an American nor an Asian brochure is selected

(iv) that either a European or an Asian brochure is selected

37 What is a mutually exclusive event?

EXPECTED VALUE AND DECISION-MAKING

38 The local council are considering purchasing a snow plough which would cost $20,000 per annum. This would save on outside contractors but the amount would depend on the severity of the winter.

Winter	Annual savings	Probability
severe	$40,000	0.2
average	$20,000	0.5
mild	$10,000	0.3

Based on the expected cost due to weather conditions, would you advise the council to buy their own plough?

39 A market trader has the choice of selling umbrellas or ice cream. It has a 60% chance of raining and a 40% chance of being fair. If it rains he will make $200 profit on umbrellas and lose $50 if he chooses ice cream. If it is fair, he will lose $10 selling umbrellas and make $150 selling ice cream. Which product would you advise him to sell?

40 A new product is expected to generate the following profits:

Level of demand	Profits	Probability
high	$100,000	0.1
medium	$50,000	0.5
low	$20,000 loss	0.4

(i) What is the expected profit from the new product?

(ii) What is the maximum you would invest in this product?

41 EXPECTED VALUES

A State two advantages of expected values.

B State two disadvantages of expected values.

PRACTICE QUESTIONS : SECTION 1

42 A company is deciding between three projects A, B and C. The expected profit from each one is as follows:

Project A		Project B		Project C	
Profit	Probability	Profit	Probability	Profit	Probability
$5,000	0.5	$10,000	0.3	$6,000	0.4
$2,500	0.5	$1,000	0.7	$4,000	0.6

Rank projects in descending order, stating expected values of each.

43 In a forthcoming sales promotion each pack of cigarettes is to contain a leaflet with eight 'scratch off' square patches, randomly arranged. The purchaser will scratch off one patch to reveal the value of a small prize. The value of the eight patches on the leaflet is to be as follows:

Value of prize	$0.20	$0.50	$1
Number of patches	5	2	1

The company has to decide on the number of packs in which to put leaflets, given a budget of $75,000.

Find the 'average cost' of a leaflet, and deduce the number of leaflets you would use and why.

44 In another promotion for cigarettes, a leaflet pictures a roulette wheel with 37 numbers, seven of which are randomly arranged winning numbers. The purchaser is allowed to scratch off seven of the 37 numbers in the hope of winning a prize. It is therefore possible to select 0, 1, 2, 3, 4, 5, 6 or 7 winning numbers on each leaflet.

(i) What is the probability of a purchase not winning a prize?

(ii) If there are one million purchases during the promotion, what are the chances of the 'Super Prize' (the Super Prize is when all seven selections are winners) being won?

45 A golf club has to decide how many programmes to produce for a Charity Pro-Am golf tournament. From previous experience of similar tournaments, it is expected that the probability of sales will be as follows:

Number of programmes demanded	Probability of demand
1,000	0.1
2,000	0.4
3,000	0.2
4,000	0.2
5,000	0.1

The best quotation from a local printer is $2,000 plus 10 pence per copy. Advertising revenue totals $1,500. Programmes are sold for 60 pence each. Unsold programmes are worthless.

Draw up a profit table with programme production levels as columns and programme demand levels as rows.

SUMMARISING AND ANALYSING DATA

PRESENTATION OF DATA

46 In constructing graphs and diagrams, state six principles which should be followed.

(i)

(ii)

(iii)

(iv)

(v)

(vi)

47 State three types of bar charts.

(i)

(ii)

(iii)

48 A farmer has land extending to 100 acres which comprises 43% wheat, 20% barley, 16% grass, 12% oats and 9% fallow. If these figures were drawn in a pie chart what would be the angle of each?

49 United won the league last season using 20 players. There were 40 league games.

Players who played	Frequency
35–40 games	1
30–34 games	3
25–29 games	4
20–24 games	5
15–19 games	1
10–14 games	2
less than 10 games	4

Construct a frequency distribution showing the number of times players played.

PRACTICE QUESTIONS : SECTION 1

50 There are 100 packets of biscuits in a box with the following weights and frequencies

Weights	Frequency
100 and less than 110	1
110 and less than 120	2
120 and less than 130	5
130 and less than 140	11
140 and less than 150	21
150 and less than 160	20
160 and less than 170	17
170 and less than 180	11
180 and less than 190	6
190 and less than 200	6

Draw a cumulative frequency curve.

51 The following data was extracted from the annual report of XY plc.

	Annual sales ($millions)	
	2001	2002
UK	31.5	35.0
EC	33.2	47.4
USA	40.3	78.9
Australia	26.1	18.2
	131.1	179.5

Show this information

(i) in a pie chart

(ii) a component bar chart.

Questions 52–53 are based on the following data

Student marks (%)	Number of students
Over 80	2
70–79	8
60–69	15
50–59	30
40–49	25
30–39	10
20–29	10
0	100

52 From the information above construct a histogram.

53 From the information above construct a frequency polygon.

AVERAGES

54 Distinguish between

    (i) the mean

    (ii) the median

    (iii) the mode

55 State three advantages and two disadvantages of using the mean

Advantages	Disadvantages
(i)	(i)
(ii)	(ii)
(iii)	

56 Calculate the arithmetic mean of 3, 6, 7, 8, 9, 11, 13, 15

57 State four advantages and three disadvantages of using the median

Advantages	Disadvantages
(i)	(i)
(ii)	(ii)
(iii)	(iii)
(iv)	

58 Calculate the median of 3, 6, 10, 14, 17, 19 and 22.

59 State four advantages and three disadvantages of using the mode

Advantages	Disadvantages
(i)	(i)
(ii)	(ii)
(iii)	(iii)
(iv)	

60 In one over a batsman scored 4, 4, 2, 1, 0 and 4. Calculate the mode.

61 In his last two 72 hole competitions, a golfer scored 67, 71, 72, 73, 72, 69, 71, 72.

Calculate

    (i) his mean score

    (ii) his median score

    (iii) his mode score

PRACTICE QUESTIONS : **SECTION 1**

62 How can the mode be determined from a histogram?

63 There are 100 packets of biscuits in a box with the following weights and frequencies

Weights	Frequency
100 and less than 110	1
110 and less than 120	2
120 and less than 130	5
130 and less than 140	11
140 and less than 150	21
150 and less than 160	20
160 and less than 170	17
170 and less than 180	11
180 and less than 190	6
190 and less than 200	6

What is the mean weight?

VARIATION

64 Calculate the standard deviation of 3, 4, 6, 8, 9.

65 In last Saturday's football matches there were 40 games played and the information below shows the number of bookings.

Number of bookings	Frequency
1	3
2	5
3	12
4	14
5	6

Calculate the standard deviation.

66 Given the following data on Product A and Product B, what is the coefficient of variation for each product?

	Mean	Standard deviation
Product A	5.46	1.29
Product B	16.38	4.21

67 The value of sales in Jimmy Farish's shop was

January	8,000	July	6,200
February	7,500	August	8,100
March	8,200	September	8,200
April	9,100	October	8,100
May	8,500	November	8,400
June	8,400	December	10,000

From this data calculate the standard deviation.

PAPER C03 : FUNDAMENTALS OF BUSINESS MATHEMATICS

Questions 68–71 are based on the following data

The numbers in seconds show the lap times of 40 drivers.

126	120	122	105	129	119	131	138
125	127	113	112	130	122	134	136
128	126	117	114	120	123	127	140
124	127	114	111	116	131	128	137
127	122	106	127	116	135	142	130

68 Group the data into eight classes.

69 Calculate the median value

70 Calculate the mean of this frequency distribution.

71 Calculate the standard deviation.

THE NORMAL DISTRIBUTION

72 State five features of a normal distribution curve.

(i)

(ii)

(iii)

(iv)

(v)

73 Give three examples where a normal distribution might appear in real life.

(i)

(ii)

(iii)

74 A group of workers have a weekly wage which is normally distributed with a mean of $400 and a standard deviation of $60. What is the probability of a worker earning.

(i) more than $430

(ii) less than $350

(iii) more than $460

(iv) between $350 and $430

(v) between $430 and $460?

75 The Island of Dreams has a temperature which is normally distributed with a mean of 70° and a standard deviation of 5°. What is the probability of

    A   (i)   the temperature below 60°

           (ii) no lower than 65°

           (iii) higher than 85°

           (iv) between 67° and 74°

    B   What is the maximum temperature that has no more than a 1% chance of being exceeded?

76 The mean weight of a bag of crisps is 50 g and a standard deviation of 10 g. What is the probability that a sample of 100 packets will have a mean of less than 48 g?

INTERRELATIONSHIP BETWEEN VARIABLES

CORRELATION AND REGRESSION

Questions 77–78 are based on the following data

Records have been kept over eight quarters of the power costs of a central heating system and the hours used, as follows

Period	Hours used	Power costs
1	25	124
2	22	131
3	16	98
4	12	74
5	7	56
6	8	65
7	15	114
8	12	86

77 (a) Using the method of least squares, calculate the fixed elements of cost,

    (b) Calculate the variable elements of cost.

78 If the coefficient of determination is 0.87, what does this signify?

PAPER C03 : FUNDAMENTALS OF BUSINESS MATHEMATICS

Questions 79–80 are based on the following data

Fertiliser (kg used)	Yield (tonnes)
100	40
200	45
300	50
400	65
500	70
600	70
700	80

79 Complete the regression line $y = ?$

80 Calculate the correlation coefficient.

81 The following table shows the ranking of six students in two tests.

Student	Maths test	English test
A	4	2
B	5	3
C	2	1
D	1	4
E	3	5
F	6	6

(i) what is the correlation coefficient?

(ii) Is there?

    (a) Positive correlation

    (b) Negative correlation

    (c) Little or no correlation

The correlation coefficient, r, depicts the linear relationship between two variables.

82 (i) for a perfect correlation $r =$

    (ii) for a perfect negative correlation $r =$

    (iii) for no correlation $r =$

83 A company's weekly costs $c were plotted against production levels (P) and a regression line calculated to be C = $1,000 + $7.5 g. Calculate the total cost if 5,000 units were produced.

84 Reject rates achieved by 100 factory operatives is to be found by the regression equation $y = 20 - 0.25x$ where y = % of reject rates and x the months of experience. What would be the predicted reject rate for an operator with one year's experience?

PRACTICE QUESTIONS : SECTION 1

Questions 85–86 are based on the following data

You are asked to investigate the relationship between what a tyre company spend on rubber and their production. You are given information over the past ten months.

Month	1	2	3	4	5	6	7	8	9	10
Production X 000 units	30	20	10	60	40	25	13	50	44	28
Rubber costs Y $000	10	11	6	18	13	10	10	20	17	15

85 Complete the regression line $y = $.

86 If production is budgeted for 15,000 units and 55,000 units for the next two months, how much is likely to be spent on rubber?

FORECASTING

TIME SERIES

87 An inflation index and a sales index of a company's sales for the last year are as follows:

Quarter	1	2	3	4
Sales index	109	120	132	145
Inflation index	100	110	121	133

Calculate the real value of sales for quarter 4.

88 Give an example of one of the following

(i)   long-term trend

(ii) cyclical variation

(iii) seasonal variation

(iv) random variation

89 In an additive time series model A = T + C + S + R, the initials stand for

(i)   A

(ii) T

(iii) C

(iv) S

(v)   R

PAPER C03 : FUNDAMENTALS OF BUSINESS MATHEMATICS

Questions 90–93 are based on the following data

The takings (in 000s) at Mr Li's Takeaway for the past 16 quarters are as follows:

Quarter	1	2	3	4
2000	13	22	58	23
2001	16	28	61	25
2002	17	29	61	26
2003	18	30	65	29

90 Calculate the four quarterly moving averages.

91 Calculate the trend.

92 Calculate the quarterly variation.

93 If Mr Li thinks his takings for the four quarters in 2004 will be $19,000, $32,000, $65,000 and $30,000, has the upward trend continued?

94 A product has a constant trend in its sales and is subject to the following quarterly seasonal variations.

Quarter	Q1	Q2	Q3	Q4
Seasonality	+50%	+50%	–50%	–50%

Assuming a multiplicative model for the time series, what should sales be for quarter 3, if sales in last quarter, Q^2, were 240?

95 Based on the last 18 periods, the underlying sales trend is $y = 345 - 1.5x$. If the seasonal factor for period 19 is –23.5, if we assume an additive forecasting model, what is the forecast for period 19?

96 Over the past 15 months, sales have had an underlying linear trend of $y = 7.5 + 3.8x$ where y is the number of items sold and x is the month of sale. Month 16 is expected to be 1.12 times the trend value.

What is the sales forecast for month 19?

FINANCIAL MATHEMATICS

97 A boy is given $100 from his grandmother on the 1st January each year. On 31st December simple interest is credited at 10% which he withdraws to spend. How much will be in the account on 31st December after five years?

98 If the boy kept the interest and credited it to his account each year, how much would be in the account on 31st December after five years if $100 was invested in year 1 but no more payments received after that?

PRACTICE QUESTIONS : SECTION 1

99 A new machine costs $5,000 and is depreciated by 8% per annum. What is the book value of the machine after five years?

100 A new machine costs $8,000 and lasts 10 years and has a scrap value of $100. What is the annual rate of compound depreciation?

101 Dougie is saving to pay for his daughter's wedding in five years' time. He puts $400 per year in the bank which will earn interest at 9%. The wedding is expected to cost $3,000. Will he have saved up enough by then?

102 How much needs to be invested now at 6% per annum to provide an annuity of $5,000 per annum for ten years commencing in five years' time?

103 Calculate the annual repayment on a bank loan of $50,000 over eight years at 9% per annum.

104 How much needs to be invested now at 5% to yield an annual income of $10,000 in perpetuity?

105 An initial investment of $2,000 yields yearly cash flows of $500, $500, $600, $600 and $440 at the end of each year. At the end of year five, there is no scrap value. If capital is available at 12%, using discounted cash flow and internal rate of return assess whether the project should be accepted.

106 If a credit card company has an annual percentage rate (APR) of 30% how much interest are they charging a customer each month?

SPREADSHEETS

107 What formula should be entered into the appropriate cell in the following worksheet to calculate the median number of televisions sold to one decimal place? How would it change if the mode was required?

	A	B	C	D	E
1	Average weekly televisions sold				
2	36	32	33	33	
3	33	38	35	37	
4	35	39	36	36	
5	32	37	37	32	
6	38	34	38	34	
7	35	35	34	37	
8					
9					
10					

PAPER C03 : FUNDAMENTALS OF BUSINESS MATHEMATICS

108 Complete the formula to be entered into cell C4 to calculate the compound interest rate if it is to be copied into cells C5 to C8?

	A	B	C	D	E
1	Investment amount	450000			
2	Interest rate	9%			
3					
4	Year number	1			
5		2			
6		3			
7		4			
8		5			
9					
10					

109

	A	B	C	D	E
1	Amount invested	−250000			
2	Cash flow year 1	90000			
3	Cash flow year 2	35000			
4	Cash flow year 3	52000			
5	Cash flow year 4	19000			
6					
7	Fixed cost of capital	5%			
8					
9					
10					

(i) What is the Excel function and formulae required to calculate the NPV on the above investment?

(ii) Rewrite the formula to calculate the IRR (assuming a figure of 10% will be used for your first guess). You are not required to fix any cell references.

110 The following calculations need to be performed in an Excel spreadsheet.

(i) $38 \div 3 \times 42.3^2$ to three decimal places

(ii) $\sqrt{220} \times 4^2$ to the nearest whole number

What should be entered in the appropriate cells in the worksheet?

111 What linear regression formula should be entered into cell C2 to forecast the growth of plants for a given level of rainfall if it is to be copied into cells C3 to C7?

	A	B	C	D	E
1	Rainfall (mm)	Plant growth (cm)			
2	30	110			
3	34	115			
4	38	115			
5	30	110			
6	42	120			
7	50	120			
8					

112 List five principles of good spreadsheet design

113 Define the following terms:

(i) Cells

(ii) Workbooks

(iii) Worksheets

(iv) Macros

114 What is the difference between formatting a cell to two decimal places and using the — ROUND function with '2' after the required function?

115 What is a template of a business plan? What advantages would it provide?

116 List the Business Mathematics functions that you remember that can be performed in Excel?

117 A chain of regional garden centres has been monitoring the relationship between sales figures and advertising spend. The following information has been established:

	A	B	C	D	
1	Region	Advertising spend $(000s)	Sales revenue $(000s)		
2	North West	12.5	31.25		
3	North East	14.3	30.03		
4	Midlands	16.7	37.91		
5	South East	14.4	33.12		
6	South West	11.7	24.57		
7	London	13.5	25.52		

Run through the key steps you would need to follow, in order to create a line of least squares in Excel.

PAPER C03 : FUNDAMENTALS OF BUSINESS MATHEMATICS

118 A local scout group has traditionally put together its budgets for various sections (beavers, cubs and scouts) on paper and then used them to draw up a group budget for approval by the Executive Committee. Recently, a fund-raising event raised enough money for a group laptop and it has been agreed that the budgets will now be drawn up using Excel. The section leaders are not sure what Excel can do and are concerned that they will now have significant extra work to do every year.

You are the treasurer of the scout group, so it has fallen to you to explain the benefits to the group that this method will bring and to suggest how the section leaders might best go about preparing their budgets so that they can minimise the work needed.

Write brief notes for the next group meeting which explain:

(a) The benefits of using Excel

(b) How the budgets can be drawn up to reduce the workload

You can assume that the leaders understand basic Excel terminology

119 Your firm is planning an investment which will cost $50,000 immediately. It should return cash flows over the next 5 years of $12,000, $15,000, $14,000, $22,000 and $18,000 respectively.

(a) Find the NPV at a cost of capital of 10% and advise the firm whether to accept the project on this basis

(b) Find the IRR and advise the firm whether to accept the project on this basis

(c) Enter the data into the blank spreadsheet below and show the formula needed to calculate the NPV and IRR using Excel.

	A	B
1		
2		
3		
4		
5		
6		
7		
8		
9		
10		
11	NPV =	
12	IRR =	

Section 2

OBJECTIVE TEST QUESTIONS

BASIC MATHEMATICS

FORMULAE

1. $6a + 6b + 2a - 3b$ is equal to

    A $6a + 3b$

    B $12ab - 6ab$

    C $12a - 18b$

    D $8a + 3b$

2. $3a^3 \times 4a^4$ is equal to

    A $12a^7$

    B $12a^{12}$

    C $7a^7$

    D $7a^{12}$

3. The number 8^{-2} is equal to

    A -16

    B 6

    C $\sqrt{8}$

    D $\dfrac{1}{64}$

4. The number $36^{-0.5}$ is equal

    A 18

    B 9

    C 6

    D $\dfrac{1}{6}$

PAPER C03 : FUNDAMENTALS OF BUSINESS MATHEMATICS

5 In the statement

Z < X < Y which of the following statements is incorrect?

A   Z is greater than X but less than Y

B   Y is greater than both X and Z

C   X is greater than Z

D   Z is lower than both X and Y

6 The correct answer to the sum 4 + 3 − 2 × (8 - 3) is

A   37

B   25

C   -3

D   -6

7 The statement $X \leq Y$ is equivalent to

A   X is less than Y

B   X is less than or equal to Y

C   X is greater than Y

D   X is greater than or equal to Y

8 If $a = 2$ and $b = 3$, $x = 7$ and $y = 8$

Then $\frac{a}{x} + \frac{b}{y}$ is equal to

A $\frac{37}{56}$

B $\frac{2}{9}$

C $\frac{14}{28}$

D $\frac{5}{15}$

9 The numeric value of the expression

$\frac{(x^3)^3}{x^7}$ when $x = 5$ is

A   0

B   5

C   25

D   125

10   Which of the following operations will not affect the order in which the numbers appear?

   A   addition and multiplication
   B   addition and subtraction
   C   subtraction and division
   D   division and multiplication

PERCENTAGES, RATIOS AND PROPORTIONS

11   Equipment is sold for $240 and makes a profit of 20% on cost. What is the profit price?

   A $10
   B $20
   C $30
   D $40

12   If sales are $500 per week and cost of sales are $300 per week, gross profit expressed as a percentage is

   A   10%
   B   20%
   C   30%
   D   40%

13   Alex, Dave and John are in partnership and profits are split in the ratio 7:6:5. If profit for the year is $36,000, how much does Alex receive?

   A $10,000
   B $12,000
   C $14,000
   D $16,000

14   If the population of Westend on Sea is 278,000 and 54,000 are of school age, what proportion of the population is of school age?

   A   15%
   B   19%
   C   23%
   D   28%

PAPER C03 : FUNDAMENTALS OF BUSINESS MATHEMATICS

15 An article in a sales catalogue is priced at $298 including VAT at 17.5%. The ex-VAT price of the product is

    A $247.34

    B $253.62

    C $255.00

    D $280.50

16 $x\%$ of 200 equals

    A $\dfrac{x}{200}$

    B $x^{1/2}$

    C $200 - x$

    D $2x$

17 What is the value of 10.37951 to two decimal places?

    A   10.4

    B   10.3

    C   10.37

    D   10.38

18 Three years ago Smith Bros. purchased a van for $12,000. If they depreciate the vehicle by 25% on a reducing balance basis, the value of the vehicle at the end of year 3 is

    A $6,000

    B $5,550.75

    C $5,062.50

    D $4,750.25

19 An audit team is made up of a manager, two seniors and four juniors. If there are 10 managers, 15 seniors and 20 juniors how many different audit teams could be formed from these numbers?

    A   20

    B   505,325

    C   5,087,250

    D   impossible to determine

OBJECTIVE TEST QUESTIONS : SECTION 2

20 City and United play each other twice over the season. Using the terms win, draw and lose, how many permutations are there in the results for the games?

    A   2

    B   6

    C   9

    D   12

ACCURACY AND ROUNDING

21 A product was priced at $117.58 and has been reduced to $105.26. To two decimal places the percentage reduction in price was

    A   9.52%

    B   9.93%

    C   10.00%

    D   10.48%

22 A CIMA class has 115 students in 2002, it increased to 167 in 2004, what is the average annual percentage increase? (accurate to 3 d.p.)

    A   15.03%

    B   17.05%

    C   20.51%

    D   22.61%

23 A skirt was sold for $85.00 (including VAT 17.5%), now VAT rate dropped to 15%. What is the new price? (round to 2 d.p)

    A $83.19

    B $72.25

    C $82.88

    D $85.00

EQUATIONS AND GRAPHS

24 A square-ended rectangular box has a volume of 1,458 cm^3. The length of the box is twice that of one side of the square end. One side of the square end measures

    A   6 cm

    B   9 cm

    C   18 cm

    D   24 cm

PAPER C03: FUNDAMENTALS OF BUSINESS MATHEMATICS

Questions 25–27 are based on the following information

The marketing department estimates that if the selling price of the new product is set at $40 per unit, sales will be 400 units per week. If the selling price is $20 per unit, sales will be 800 units per week. The production department estimates that variable costs will be $7.50 per unit and fixed costs $10,000 per week.

25 The cost equation is

    A $10,000 + $7.5x

    B $10,000 − $7.5x

    C $10,000 + $40

    D $10,000 + $75x

26 The sales revenue equation is

    A   400 − 9

    B   1,200 − 9

    C $60x - \dfrac{x^2}{20}$

    D $60x - x^2$

27 The profit equation is

    A $-\dfrac{x^2}{20} + 52.5x - 10,000$

    B $-x\,52.5 - 10,000$

    C $x^2 - 52.5x + 10,000$

    D $x^2 - 52.5x - 10,000$

28 If 3x + 4y − 25 and 10x + 2y − 38 what are the values of x and y?

    A   x = 3   y = 3

    B   x = 3   y = 4

    C   x = 4   y = 5

    D   x = 5   y = 4

29 If $9x^2 - 30x + 25 = 0$ then x is equal to

    A $\dfrac{2}{3}$

    B   1

    C $\dfrac{5}{3}$

    D   2

OBJECTIVE TEST QUESTIONS : SECTION 2

30 The shape of a graph of linear equation will be

    A   U shape

    B   straight line

    C   L shape

    D   depends on the linear equation

31 For the equation $ax^2 + bx + c = 0$, if $b^2 - 4ac$ is positive then

    A   there is only one solution

    B   there are two possible solutions

    C   there are no real solutions

    D   impossible to determine without knowing their values

32 In the equations

$2x + 3y + 4z = 9$

$3x - 2y - 3z = 3$

$4x + 5y - 2z = 25$

the values of x, y and z are

    A   x = 2   y = 3   z = -1

    B   x = 1   y = 3   z = 2

    C   x = 2   y = 1   z = 3

    D   x = 3   y = 2   z = 1

33 If $6x^2 + 12x = 4(5x + 2)$ then the values of x are

    A $\frac{-2}{3}$ or 2

    B $\frac{-3}{2}$ or 1

    C $\frac{-3}{2}$ or 1

    D $\frac{2}{3}$ or 2

PROBABILITY

PROBABILITY THEORY

Questions 34–37 relate to the following information

A pack of cards consists of 52 playing cards.

34 What is the probability that a card selected at random is the ace of hearts?

    A   1 in 2

    B   1 in 13

    C   1 in 26

    D   1 in 52

35 A bag contains 10 balls, with 3 red ones, 4 blue ones and 3 yellow ones. What is the probability of getting blues – red – yellow in the first three attempts.

    A   0.001

    B   0.037

    C   0.036

    D   0.028

36 What is the probability that a card selected at random is a heart?

    A   1 in 2

    B   1 in 4

    C   1 in 9

    D   1 in 13

37 Draw a dice (six sides) and toss a coin at the same time, what is the probability of getting a 6 and Head.

    A $\frac{1}{36}$

    B $\frac{2}{3}$

    C $\frac{1}{4}$

    D $\frac{1}{12}$

OBJECTIVE TEST QUESTIONS : SECTION 2

Questions 38–41 relate to a number of CIMA students who recently sat for Paper 03

Type of student	Total number of scripts	Total number of passes
Male	1,000	500
Female	500	300

38 If a student is selected at random what is the probability she is female?

    A   1 in 2

    B   1 in 3

    C   1 in 4

    D   1 in 5

39 If a student is selected at random what is the probability that they failed?

    A   1 in 2

    B   1 in 3

    C   7 in 15

    D   8 in 15

40 If a student is selected at random what is the probability that the student is male or someone who failed?

    A   0.5

    B   0.6

    C   0.7

    D   0.8

41 If a student is selected at random what is the probability of selecting a male who failed?

    A   1 in 2

    B   1 in 3

    C   1 in 4

    D   1 in 5

Questions 42 and 43 are based on the following

A CIMA class has 90 students, with 60 of them are male. Among these 60 male students, 20 of them are taking CFA course at the same time. The CFA class has a total of 75 students.

PAPER C03 : FUNDAMENTALS OF BUSINESS MATHEMATICS

42 What is the probability that a student is random selected from these two classes is either male or taking a CFA course?

    A $0.45 \left(\dfrac{75}{90+75} \right)$

    B $0.36 \left(\dfrac{60}{90+75} \right)$

    C $0.82 \left(\dfrac{60+75}{90+75} \right)$

    D $0.7 \left(\dfrac{60+75-20}{90+75} \right)$

43 Three cards are chosen at random from a deck without replacement, what is the probability of getting a Jack, a ten and a nine in order?

    A $\dfrac{8}{16,575}$

    B $\dfrac{1}{2,197}$

    C $\dfrac{6}{35.152}$

    D $\dfrac{1}{8}$

EXPECTED VALUE AND DECISION-MAKING

44 A retailer has the choice of selling Product A which has a 0.4 chance of high sales and a 0.6 chance of low sales. High sales would yield a profit of $600. Low sales would yield a profit of $100. If Product B was sold there is a 0.6 chance of high sales and a 0.4 chance of low sales which would result in a profit of $400 or a loss of $50. Which product would be chosen and what would be the expected value?

    A   Product A $300

    B   Product B $220

    C   Product A $220

    D   Product B $300

45 Ten per cent of golf balls have a minor defect. They are packaged in boxes of six. What is the probability that a box selected at random has no defects?

    A   0.41

    B   0.45

    C   0.51

    D   0.53

OBJECTIVE TEST QUESTIONS : SECTION 2

46 If the three possible outcomes of a decision are profits of $10, $50 and $80 with probabilities of 0.3, 0.3 and 0.4, what is the expected profit?

- A $40
- B $44
- C $47
- D $50

47 A supermarket is opening a new store and they have identified two sites A and B with 0.8 chance of making $400,000 profit per annum and a 0.2 chance of incurring an $80,000 loss. The expected value of those sites is

- A $300,000
- B $302,000
- C $304,000
- D $306,000

48 A newspaper vendor buys daily newspapers each day which have a resale value at the end of the day of zero. He buys the papers for 15p and sells them for 30p. The levels of demand per day and their associated probabilities are as follows

Demand per day	Probability
400	0.2
440	0.3
480	0.4
520	0.1

How many newspapers should the vendor buy each day?

- A 400
- B 440
- C 480
- D 520

49 A social club has a lottery draw based on numbers between 1 and 40. If they pay $50 for the winning number and there are no other expenses how much will they need to sell each ticket for in order to make $50 profit?

- A $2
- B $2.50
- C $3
- D not enough information given

PAPER C03 : FUNDAMENTALS OF BUSINESS MATHEMATICS

50 If a roulette table has 37 numbers 0-36 and pays odds of 35-1 on punters guessing the correct number, what is the expected rate of return on a $100 investment?

- A −5%
- B +5%
- C 95%
- D 100%

51 A new car is worth $20,000. The probability of this car being stolen or being involved in an accident over a year is 1%.

The driver pays an insurance policy of $500 per annum. The annual expected value to the insurance company is

- A $500
- B $400
- C $300
- D $200

SUMMARISING AND ANALYSING DATA

PRESENTATION OF DATA

52 Which of the following statements is correct?

- A data + data = information
- B data + information = meaning
- C data + meaning = information
- D information + meaning = data

53 In a histogram in which one class interval is one and a half times as wide as the remaining classes, the height to be plotted in relation to the frequency for that class is

- A × 0.67
- B × 0.75
- C × 1
- D × 1.5

54 In a pie chart, if wages are represented by 90° and the total cost is $550,000, what is the amount paid out in wages?

- A $135,000
- B $137,500
- C $142,000
- D $145,000

55 Cumulative frequencies are plotted against

    A   the mid-point

    B   the lower class boundaries

    C   the upper class boundaries

    D   any of the above

56 A frequency distribution of a sample of monthly incomes is as follows

$	Frequency
400 and less than 800	7
800 and less than 1,000	16
1,000 and less than 1,200	28
1,200 and less than 1,300	21
1,300 and less than 1,400	8
	80

If the area between $800 and $1,000 has a height of 8 cm, what is the height of the rectangle 1,000 and less than 1,200?

    A   10

    B   12

    C   14

    D   16

57 Which of the following are types of bar chart?

    (i)   simple

    (ii)   multiple

    (iii)   component

    (iv)   compound

    A   (i) and (ii)

    B   (i), (ii), (iv)

    C   (i), (ii), (iii)

    D   (i), (ii), (iii), (iv)

58 A histogram uses a set of rectangles to represent a grouped frequency table. To be correctly presented, the histogram must show the relationship of the rectangles to the frequencies by reference to the

    A   height of each rectangle

    B   area of each rectangle

    C   width of each rectangle

    D   diagonal of each rectangle

PAPER C03 : FUNDAMENTALS OF BUSINESS MATHEMATICS

AVERAGES

59 The arithmetic mean of 3, 6, 10, 14, 17, 19 and 22 is

   A   11
   B   13
   C   14
   D   15

60 The median of 3, 6, 10, 14, 17, 19 and 22 is

   A   11
   B   13
   C   14
   D   15

61 The mean weight of 10 parcels is 20 kg. If the individual weights in kilograms are 15, x, 22, 14, 21, 15, 20, x, 18, 27 then the value of x is

   A   20 kg
   B   24 kg
   C   40 kg
   D   48 kg

62 The mode is the value

   A   which appears with the highest frequency
   B   which is the same as the arithmetic mean
   C   which is the mid-point value
   D   none of the above

63 A factory employs staff in four departments for which the average mean wage per employee per week is as follows

Department	W	X	Y	Z
Mean wage	$50	$100	$70	$80
No. of employees	20	5	10	5

The average mean wage per employee is

   A $60
   B $65
   C $70
   D $75

64 If there are *n* items in the distribution the value of the median is

    A $\dfrac{n+1}{2}$

    B $\dfrac{n-1}{2}$

    A   n + 1

    A   n − 1

Questions 65–67 are based on the following data

A sample of 12 packets of crisps taken from a box had the following weights in grams 504, 506, 501, 505, 507, 506, 504, 508, 503, 505, 502, 504.

65 Calculate the mean weight.

    A   502.3

    B   503.4

    C   504.6

    D   505.7

66 Calculate the median weight.

    A   504

    B   504.5

    C   505

    D   505.5

67 Calculate the modal weight.

    A   504

    B   505

    C   506

    D   507

68 Which of the following is *not* an advantage of the median?

    A   It is simple to understand

    B   It is not affected by extreme values

    C   It can be the value of an actual item in the distribution

    D   It is suitable for use in mathematical statistics

VARIATION

69 Several groups of invoices are being analysed. For each group the coefficient of variation has been calculated. The coefficient of variation measures

- A the range of values between the invoices
- B the correlation between the invoice values
- C the relative dispersion of the invoice values
- D the variation between the sample mean and the true mean

70 The standard deviation of 3, 5, 8, 11 and 13 is

- A 3.69
- B 4.25
- C 5.41
- D 7.62

71 If the standard deviation is 1.1 and the arithmetic mean is 3.5 then the coefficient of variation is equal to

- A 29.86
- B 31.43
- C 33.79
- D 34.61

72 Four products have the same mean weight of 250 grams but their standard deviates are

Product A	10 grams
Product B	15 grams
Product C	20 grams
Product D	25 grams

Which product has the highest coefficient of variation?

- A Product A
- B Product B
- C Product C
- D Product D

OBJECTIVE TEST QUESTIONS : SECTION 2

THE NORMAL DISTRIBUTION

Questions 73–79 are based on the following information

A group of workers have a weekly wage which is normally distributed with a mean of $360 per week and a standard deviation of $15.

73 What is the probability a worker earns more than $380?

    A   4%

    B   5%

    C   7%

    D   9%

74 What is the probability a worker earns less than $330?

    A   1%

    B   2%

    C   3%

    D   4%

75 What is the probability a worker earns more than $420?

    A   5%

    B   4%

    C   2%

    D   0%

76 What is the probability a worker earns between $330 and $390?

    A   50%

    B   75%

    C   90%

    D   95%

77 What is the probability a worker earns between $370 and $400?

    A   1%

    B   15%

    C   20%

    D   25%

PAPER C03 : FUNDAMENTALS OF BUSINESS MATHEMATICS

78 What are the limits which enclose the middle 98%?

    A $330.60 and $389.40

    B $325.05 and $394.95

    C $320.40 and $400.40

    D $300 and $450

79 A normal distribution has a mean of 150 and a standard deviation of 20. Eighty per cent of this distribution is below

    A   150

    B   154.8

    C   159.6

    D   166.8

80 In a normal distribution with a mean of 150, 6.68% of the population is above 180. The standard deviation of the distribution is

    A   10

    B   15

    C   20

    D   25

81 Which of the following is not a feature of a normal distribution?

    A   It is symmetrical

    B   It is bell-shaped

    C   The mean is equal to the mode

    D   The mean is above the median

INDEX NUMBERS

82 An inflation index and index numbers of a company's sales ($) for the last year are given below.

Quarter:	1	2	3	4
Sales ($) index:	109	120	132	145
Inflation index:	100	110	121	133

'Real' sales, i.e. adjusted for inflation, are:

    A   approximately constant and keeping up with inflation

    B   growing steadily and not keeping up with inflation

    C   growing steadily and keeping ahead of inflation

    D   falling steadily and not keeping up with inflation

OBJECTIVE TEST QUESTIONS : SECTION 2

83 Four years ago material X cost $5 per kg and the price index most appropriate to the cost of material X stood at 150. The same index now stands at 430.

What is the best estimate of the current cost of material X per kg?

A $1.74

B $9.33

C $14.33

D $21.50

84 Two years ago the price index appropriate to the cost of material X had a value of 120. It now has a value of 160.

If material X costs $2,000/kg today, what would its cost/kg have been two years ago?

A $1,500

B $1,667

C $2,667

D $3,200

85 Details of an index number are given below:

Group	Base	Weight	Index
Food & Drink	100	50	140
Travel & Leisure	100	30	130
Housing	100	20	120
All items	100	100	??

The All items index number is closest to:

A   130

B   133

C   135

D   146

86 An index number is made up of two items, food and non-food.

Sub-group	Weight	Index
Non-food	7	130
Food	3	?
All items	10	127

The index number for the sub-group Food is closest to:

A   120

B   122

C   124

D   126

87 In 2000, a price index based on 1990 = 100 had a value of x.

During 2000, it was re-based at 2000 = 100, and in 2008 the new index stood at 112. If the total price movement between 1990 and 2008 was an increase of 40%, what was the value of x in 2000, i.e. before re-basing?

- A 125
- B 128
- C 136
- D 140

88 The price index for a commodity in the current year is 87 (base year =100) and the current price is £490 per unit.

What was the price in the base year?

- A £462.30
- B £553.70
- C £563.22
- D £577.00

INTERRELATIONSHIP BETWEEN VARIABLES

CORRELATION AND REGRESSION

89 If $\Sigma x = 560$ $\Sigma y = 85$ $\Sigma x^2 = 62,500$

$\Sigma xy = 14,200$ and $n = 12$, the regression line of y on x is equal to

- A $-0.281 + 6.03x$
- B $-6.03 + 0.281x$
- C $0.281 + 6.03x$
- D $6.03 + 0.281x$

90 In a forecasting model based on $y = a + bx$, the intercept is $234. If the value of y is $491 and $x = 20$ then b is equal to

- A 12.25
- B 12.85
- C 13.35
- D 13.95

91 A company's weekly costs $C were plotted against production levels for the last 50 weeks and a regression line C = 1,000 + 250p was found. This would denote that

  A   fixed costs are $1,250

  B   variable costs are $1,250

  C   fixed costs are $1,000; variable costs $2.50

  D   fixed costs are $250; variable costs are $1,000

92 The following table shows the ranking of six students in their CIMA Economics and CIMA Business Mathematics

Student	Economics	Maths rank
A	4	2
B	5	3
C	2	1
D	1	4
E	3	5
F	6	6

What is the correlation between the two subjects?

  A   0.31

  B   0.33

  C   0.35

  D   0.37

93 Management accountants require to calculate costs. The variable to be predicted is known as the

  A   dependent variable

  B   statistical variable

  C   independent variable

  D   high-low variable

94 What type of relationship would there likely be between the cost of electricity and electricity production levels?

  A   perfect positive linear

  B   perfect negative linear

  C   high positive

  D   low negative

PAPER C03 : FUNDAMENTALS OF BUSINESS MATHEMATICS

95 The coefficient of determination (r^2) explains the

- A percentage variation in the coefficient of correlation
- B percentage variation in the dependent variable which is explained by the independent variable
- C percentage variation in the independent variable which is explained by the dependent variable
- D extent of the casual relationship between the two variables

96 In a forecast model based on y = a + bx, the interest is $234. If the value of y is $491 and x is 20 then the value of the slope =

- A −4.55
- B −12.85
- C 12.85
- D 24.85

97 In the equation y = a + bx, a is equal to

- A the intercept
- B the gradient
- C the regression line
- D the coefficient

98 If there is a perfect positive correlation between two variables then the value of R, the correlation coefficient is

- A greater than 1
- B equal to 1
- C equal to 0
- D equal to −1

FORECASTING

TIME SERIES

99 Over an 18 month period, sales have been found to have an underlying linear trend of y = 7.112 + 3.949x where y is the number of items sold and x represents the month. Monthly deviations from trend have been calculated and month 19 is expected to be 1.12 times the trend value. The forecast number of items to be sold in month 19 is

- A 88
- B 90
- C 92
- D 94

OBJECTIVE TEST QUESTIONS : SECTION 2

100 The influence of booms and slumps in an industry is a measure of

    A   long-term trends

    B   cyclical variations

    C   seasonal variations

    D   random variations

101 A product has a constant (flat) trend in its sales, and is subject to quarterly seasonal variations as follows:

Quarter	Q_1	Q_2	Q_3	Q_4
Seasonality	+50%	+50%	−50%	−50%

Sales last quarter, Q_2, were 240 units.

Assuming a multiplicative model for the time series, predicted unit sales for the next quarter, Q_3, will be closest to

    A   60

    B   80

    C   120

    D   160

102 The takings at Mr Li's takeaway for the first quarter of 2008 were $25,000 – the underlying trend at this point was $23,000 takings and the seasonal factor is 0.78. Assuming a multiplicative model for seasonal adjustment, the seasonally – adjusted figure for that quarter is:

    A $19,500

    B $17,940

    C $32,051

    D $29,487

FINANCIAL MATHEMATICS

103 A credit card company is charging an annual percentage rate of 25.3%. This is equivalent to a monthly rate of

    A   1.8

    B   1.9

    C   2.0

    D   2.2

PAPER C03 : FUNDAMENTALS OF BUSINESS MATHEMATICS

104 Johnny receives $1,000 per annum starting today and receives five such payments. If the rate of interest is 8% what is the net present value of this income stream?

    A $4,000
    B $4,100
    C $4,282
    D $4,312

105 A new machine costs $5,000 and is depreciated by 8% per annum. The book value of the machine in five years time will be

    A $5,000
    B $4,219
    C $3,295
    D $2,970

106 Which is worth most, at present values, assuming an annual rate of interest of 12%?

    A $1,200 one year from now
    B $1,400 two years from now
    C $1,600 three years from now
    D $1,800 four years from now

107 A landlord receives a rent of $1,000 to be received over ten successive years. The first payment is due now. If interest rates are 8% then the present value of this income is equal to

    A $6,250
    B $6,973
    C $7,247
    D $7,915

108 If interest rates are 8%, which is worth most at present values?

    A $1,200 one year from now
    B $1,400 two years from now
    C $1,600 three years from now
    D $1,800 four years from now

109 How much would need to be invested today at 6% per annum to provide an annuity of $5,000 per annum for ten years commencing in five years' time?

    A $5,000
    B $19,000
    C $29,150
    D $39,420

OBJECTIVE TEST QUESTIONS : SECTION 2

110 What is the annual repayment on a bank loan of $50,000 over eight years at 9%?

   A $8,975
   B $9,033
   C $9,214
   D $9,416

111 How much needs to be invested now at 5% to yield an annual income of $4,000 in perpetuity?

   A $80,000
   B $90,000
   C $100,000
   D $120,000

112 How much needs to be invested now at 6% to yield an annual pension income of $15,000 in perpetuity?

   A $200,000
   B $250,000
   C $300,000
   D $350,000

SPREADSHEETS

113

	A	B	C	D	E
1	Values for x	$y = x^2 + 5x + 10$			
2	−25	510			
3	−20	310			
4	−15	160			
5	−10	60			
6	−5	10			
7	0	10			
8	5	60			
9	10	160			
10	15	310			
11	20	510			

The above data is to be plotted onto a labelled graph in Excel.

What shape will the resulting graph be?

   A   A curve with a maximum point
   B   A straight line with a change of gradient, where $x = 0$
   C   A curve with a minimum point
   D   Curved but the number of minimum or maximum points cannot be predicted without further calculations

PAPER C03 : FUNDAMENTALS OF BUSINESS MATHEMATICS

114 The following data is to be used to create a pie chart in Excel.

	A	B	C	D	E
1			$		
2		18–25	59.3		
3		26–35	61.6		
4		36–45	10.3		
5		46–55	15.8		
6		56 and over	9.9		
7		Total	156.9		
8					
9					
10					
11					

What range should be selected?

A B2:C7

B A2:C6

C B2:C6

D The data cannot be used to create a pie chart without alteration

115 Which of the following are principles of good spreadsheet design?

(i)   Build in cross-checks to validate data/calculations

(ii) Use absolute values in formulae

(iii) Keep graphs on separate chart sheets where possible

(iv) Use colour coded fonts on larger plans

A (i) and (iii)

B (i), (ii) and (iii)

C (i), (ii), (iii) and (iv)

D (i), (iii) and (iv)

116 If the formula =NOW() is entered into an Excel spreadsheet:

A Only the current date will be displayed in the cell

B Only the current time will be displayed in the cell

C Both the current time and date will be displayed in the cell

D The display in the cell will depend on whether DATE, TIME or DATETIME is typed between the brackets

117

	A	B	C	D
1	BORROWING RATES AND LOANS			
2				
3	Loan rate (%)	Amount outstanding		Forecast
4	8.00	12,050		
5	8.25	12,600		
6	8.50	12,835		
7	8.50	12,200		
8	8.75	13,060		
9	9.00	13,500		
10	9.25	13,100		
11	9.25	13,300		
12	9.25	13,500		
13	9.50	14,100		

The formula =FORECAST(A4,$B$4:$B$13,$A$4:$A$13) is to be entered into cell D4.

A   can now be copied into cells D5 through D13, and the resulting data used to plot the line of least squares (i.e. a regression line)

B   It can now be copied into cells D5 through D13, and the resulting data used to calculate a frequency distribution

C   The formula should have the fixed cell references removed so it can then be copied into cells D5 through D13, and the resulting data used to plot the line of least squares (i.e. a regression line)

D   The formula should have the fixed cell references removed so it can then be copied into cells D5 through D13, and the resulting data used to calculate a frequency distribution

118

	A	B	C	D
1	Product line	Sales $000		
2	Soups	1,200		
3	Tinned vegetables	600		
4	Sauces	450		
5	Salad dressings	900		
6	Tinned stews	550		
7	Condiments	200		
8	Tinned pasta	1,700		
9	Total	5,600		

The above data is to be analysed.

To perform the analysis the following actions will be carried out:

1. Sort the data by descending size.
2. Calculate the percentage of the total that each item represents.
3. Find the cumulative percentage sales each item contributes.

This analysis is known as

A   Regression analysis

B   Pareto analysis

C   Frequency distribution analysis

D   Standard deviation and probability analysis

119

	A	B	C	D
1		Cash flows		
2				
3	Initial investment	350,000		
4	Year 1	60,000		
5	Year 2	95,000		
6	Year 3	120,000		
7	Year 4	180,000		
8	Year 5	200,000		
9				
10	Interest rate	0.2		
11				

Which of the following formula will correctly calculate the NPV of the above investment?

A   =NPV(B10,B4:B8)-B3

B   =NPV(B10,B4:B8)+B3

C   =NPV(B10,B3:B8)

D   =NPV(B10,SUM(-B3/B4:B8))

120

	A	B	C	D	E
1					
2	Amount invested	368,000			
3	Cash flow year 1	48,000			
4	Cash flow year 2	27,000			
5	Cash flow year 3	32,000			
6	Cash flow year 4	19,000			
7					
8	Fixed cost of capital	12%			
9					

The formula below (without the missing data) was entered into cell B10 and the answer was 0.09.

Identify the contents of the blanks in the formula =ROUND(• (B3:B6)/B2, •)

A • IRR • 1

B • AVERAGE • 2

C • NPV • 1

D • ROI •2

Section 3

ANSWERS TO PRACTICE QUESTIONS

BASIC MATHEMATICS

FORMULAE

1   (i) $(5 + 2)a + (6 - 3)b = 7a + 3b$

      (ii) $(4 + 3 - 2 - 1)x = 4x$

      (iii) $3b + 4c - 2b + 5c = b + 9c$

      (iv) $(2 + 2)a + (3 - 3)x + (-4 + 2)y = 4a - 2y$

      (v) $(3 - 4)x + (9 + 5)y + -2z = -x + 14y - 2z$

2   (i) $10x + 15y - 20z$

      (ii) $-2x - 3x^2$

      (iii) $-4x + 8y - 12z$

      (iv) $6x^2 - 12xy + 9xz$

      (v) $-24y^2 + 12yz$

3   (i) $2 \times a^{(2+3)} = 2a^5$

      (ii) $3 \times 2 \times a^{(2+3)} = 6a^5$

      (iii) $3 \times 12 \times x^{(3+4)} = 36x^7$

      (iv) $3^3 \times (a^2)^3 \times b^3 = 27a^6b^3$

      (v) $(2a^2x)^2 = 2^2 \times 2^4 \times 3^2 = 4 \times 16 = 576$

4   (i) $x^{(5-2)} = x^3$

      (ii) $x^{(9-7)} = x^2$

      (iii) $5x^{(5-4)} = 5x$

      (iv) $a^{(6-6)} = a^0 = 1$

      (v) $a^{(5-7)} = a^{-2} = 1/a^2$

5 (i) $\sqrt{3} = 1.732$

  (ii) $\sqrt{2} = 1.414$

  (iii) $\left(\sqrt{4}\right)^3 = \sqrt{64} = 8$

  (iv) $\dfrac{1}{10^3} = \dfrac{1}{1,000} = 0.001$

  (v) $\dfrac{1}{\sqrt{36}} = \dfrac{1}{6}$

6 (i) $\dfrac{15}{20} + \dfrac{8}{20} = \dfrac{23}{20} = 1\dfrac{3}{20}$

  (ii) $\dfrac{14}{16} - \dfrac{3}{16} = \dfrac{11}{16}$

  (iii) $\dfrac{1}{3} \times \dfrac{1}{5} = \dfrac{1}{15}$

  (iv) $\dfrac{3}{4} \times \dfrac{5}{2} = \dfrac{15}{8} = 1\dfrac{7}{8}$

  (v) $1\dfrac{15}{21} + 3\dfrac{14}{21} = 5\dfrac{8}{21}$

7 $\sqrt{\dfrac{2 \times 600 \times 10}{6 \times 0.2}} = 100$

So Q = 100

8 $\sqrt{\dfrac{2 \times £20 \times 24,000}{£6}} = 400$

So Q = 400

9 (i)   false
  (ii)   false
  (iii) false
  (iv)   true
  (v)   true
  (vi)   true
  (vii) true
  (viii) true
  (ix)   true
  (x)   true

ANSWERS TO PRACTICE QUESTIONS : SECTION 3

PERCENTAGES, RATIOS AND PROPORTIONS

10 (i) $17.50
 (ii) $22.34
 (iii) $29.78
 (iv) $37.23
 (v) $74.46

11 (i) Gross profit and mark-up are both $40 but margins are different.

$$GP = \frac{40}{240} = \frac{1}{6}$$

 (ii) $$\text{Mark up} = \frac{40}{200} = \frac{1}{5}$$

12 (i) $$\frac{200}{500} = \frac{2}{5}$$

 (ii) .4

 (ii) 40%

 (iv) 4:10

13 James $\frac{5}{20}$ = $12,500

 Fred $\frac{7}{20}$ = $17,500

 Martin $\frac{8}{20}$ = $20,000

14 Six different possibilities

Red	White	Blue
Red	Blue	White
White	Red	Blue
White	Blue	Red
Blue	Red	White
Blue	White	Red

15
Customer A discount 15% of 1,200	=	180
Customer B discount 12% of 650	=	78
Total discount given	=	$258

PAPER C03 : FUNDAMENTALS OF BUSINESS MATHEMATICS

16 (i) true
(ii) false
(iii) false
(iv) false
(v) true
(vi) false

ACCURACY AND ROUNDING

17 (i) continuous
(ii) discrete
(iii) independent
(iv) dependent
(v) biased
(vi) unbiased

18 32.6 + 0.05 + 4.32 + 0.05 = 36.975

(32.6 − 0.05) + (4.32 − 0.05) = 36.865

32.6 + 4.32 = 36.92

$$\frac{36.975 - 36.865}{2} = 0.055$$

so 36.92 ± 0.055

19 (32.6 + 0.05) − (4.32 − 0.05) = 28.335

(32.6 − 0.05) − (4.32 + 0.05) = 28.225

$$\frac{28.335 - 28.225}{2}$$

= 0.055   28.28 ± 0.055

20 Highest = 32.65 × 4.325 = 141.211

Lowest = 32.55 × 4.315 = 140.453

so 140.83 ± 0.38

21 $\frac{56.99 - 52.49}{56.99} \times 100 = 7.90\%$

ANSWERS TO PRACTICE QUESTIONS : SECTION 3

EQUATIONS AND GRAPHS

22 (i) $3x + 4y = 25$ multiply by 4   (1)

$4x + 5y = 32$ multiply by 3   (2)

$12x + 16y = 100$

$12x + 15y = 96$

subtracting (1) from (2) becomes $y = 4$

$3x + 16 = 25$

$x = 3$

so $x = 3, y = 4$

(ii) $x + y = 10$

$x - 4y = 0$

multiply by 4

$4x + 4y = 40$

$4x - 10y = 0$

$20y = 40$

$y = 2$

$4x + 8 = 32$

$x = 8$

(iii) $2x + 3y = 42$

$5x - y = 20$

Multiply by 5

$10x + 15y = 210$

$10x - 2y = 40$

$17y = 170$

$y = 10$

$10x + 150 = 210$

$x = 6$

(iv) $\dfrac{x}{3} + \dfrac{y}{2} = 7$ $\dfrac{2x}{3} - \dfrac{y}{6} = 7$

multiply everything by 6

$2x + 3y = 42$ (1)

$4x - y = 42$ (2)

multiply equation (2) by 3

$2x + 3y = 42$

$12x - 3y = 126$

$14x = 168$, so $x = 12$

If $x = 12$, then $y = 6$

23 $2x + 3y + 4z = 9$ (1)

$3x - 2y - 3z = 3$ (2)

$4x + 5y - 2z = 25$ (3)

Step 1 – eliminate x

$6x + 9y + 12z = 27$ equation (1) × 3

$6x - 4y - 6z = 6$ equation (2) × 2

subtract $13y + 18z = 21$ (4)

$4x + 6y + 8z = 18$ equation (1) × 2

$4x + 5y - 2z = 25$ (3)

subtract $y + 10z = -7$ (5)

multiply equation (5) by 13

$13y + 130z = -91$ (6)

$13y + 18z = 21$

$112z = -112$

z = −1 y + 10z = −7 y − 10 = −7

y = −7 + 10

y = 3

2x + 3y + 4z = 9

2x + 9 − 4 = 9

2x = 4

x = 2

solution x = 2, y = 3, z = −1

24 (i) $m(a + b) + n(a + b)$

(ii) $3am^3(4a − 5m^2)$

(iii) $(x + 6)(x − 2)$

(iv) $(5p − 2q)(2p + 3q)$

(v) $3x(x + 2)$

25 (i) $\dfrac{-(-30) \pm \sqrt{(-30)^2 - 4 \times 9 \times 25}}{2 \times 9} = \dfrac{30 \pm \sqrt{0}}{18} = \dfrac{5}{3}$

(ii) $\dfrac{-(-20) \pm \sqrt{(-20)^2 - 4 \times 3 \times (-25)}}{2 \times 3} = \dfrac{20 \pm \sqrt{700}}{6} = 7.74 \text{ or } -1.08$

(iii) $\dfrac{-6 \pm \sqrt{6^2 - 4 \times 1 \times (-16)}}{2 \times 1} = \dfrac{-6 \pm \sqrt{100}}{2} = \dfrac{-6 \pm 10}{2}$

$= -8 \text{ or } 2$

26 (i) Factorise x = 2 or 3

(ii) Does not factorise x = −1.59 or −4.41

(iii) Factorises x = 3 twice

(iv) Does not have real solutions as $(b^2 − 4ac)$ is negative

27 (i) true

(ii) true

(iii) false

(iv) true

(v) false

(vi) false

(vii) true

(viii) false

PROBABILITY

PROBABILITY THEORY

28 (i) $\dfrac{26}{52} = \dfrac{1}{2}$

(ii) $\dfrac{13}{52} = \dfrac{1}{4}$

(iii) $\dfrac{4}{52} = \dfrac{1}{13}$

(iv) $\dfrac{1}{52} = \dfrac{1}{52}$

29 (i) a priori

(ii) empirical probability

(iii) subjective probability

(iv) venn

30 He is not too over generous

In match 1 there are three possible outcomes: City win – United win – draw

In match 2 there are also three possible outcomes, so between the two matches there are nine possible outcomes, so the chances of either team beating each other twice is 9 — 1, not good odds.

31 (i) 200 in 500 or 40%

(ii) 200 + 150 in 500 or 70%

(iii) 200 + 150 + 50 in 500 or 80%

(iv) 500 – 150 in 500 or 70%

(v) 500 – (100 + 50) in 500 or 70%

32 (i) 50 in 100 or 50%

(ii) 60 in 100 or 60%

(iii) $\dfrac{50}{100} \times \dfrac{60}{100}$ or 30%

(iv) Someone who is not male or qualified is female and unqualified. This probability

$= \dfrac{50}{100} \times \dfrac{40}{100} = 20\%$

therefore male or qualified must be 100 – 20% = 80%

(v) same as (iii) $= \dfrac{50}{100} \times \dfrac{60}{100} = 30\%$

33 Where only percentage figures are given, it is easier to use an absolute number such as 1,000 and produce the following table:

	Factory X	Factory Y	Total
Fault	25	135	160
OK	225	615	840
Total	250	750	1,000

(i) 160 in 1,000 or 16%

(ii) 25 in 160 or 16%

(iii) 135 in 160 or 84%

34 There is only one colour which can be selected three times – red

(i) so $\frac{4}{7} \times \frac{3}{6} \times \frac{2}{5} = \frac{24}{210} = \frac{4}{35} = 0.11$

(ii) There are six possible outcomes that give one of each colour

(i)	Red	White	Yellow
(ii)	Red	Yellow	White
(iii)	White	Red	Yellow
(iv)	White	Yellow	Red
(v)	Yellow	Red	White
(vi)	Yellow	White	Red

So probability $= 6 \times \frac{4}{7} \times \frac{2}{6} \times \frac{1}{5}$

$= \frac{48}{210}$

$= \frac{8}{35} = 0.23$

35 (i) Probability that first toss is head

= 50 – 50 or 1 in 2

(ii) Probability

$= \frac{1}{2} \times \frac{1}{2} = 1$ in 4

(iii) If neither toss is a head then both must be a tail.

Probability of two tails

$= \frac{1}{2} \times \frac{1}{2} = 1$ in 4

so chances that neither are heads is 1 in 4

(iv) For head not to appear in three consecutive tosses, we would need 3 tails which is

$= \frac{1}{2} \times \frac{1}{2} \times \frac{1}{2} = \frac{1}{8}$

ANSWERS TO PRACTICE QUESTIONS : SECTION 3

36 (i) Probability that a European brochure is selected $= \dfrac{285}{500} = 0.57$

(ii) Probability that an African brochure is not selected

$= \dfrac{500 - 15}{500} = \dfrac{485}{500} = 0.97$

(iii) Probability that neither an American nor an Asian brochure is selected

$= \dfrac{500 - 90 - 10}{500} = \dfrac{300}{500} = 0.60$

(iv) Probability that either a European or an Asian brochure is selected

$= \dfrac{285 + 110}{500} = \dfrac{395}{500} = 0.79$

37 MUTUALLY EXCLUSIVE EVENTS

Two or more events are said to be mutually exclusive if the occurrence of any one of them precludes the occurrence of all others, that is only one thing can happen. For example if we throw a coin and it lands heads it cannot be a tail.

EXPECTED VALUE AND DECISION-MAKING

38 Cost of new machine = $20,000

Expected saving = (0.2 × 40,000) + (0.5 × 20,000) + (0.3 × 10,000)

= $8,000 + $10,000 + $3,000

= $21,000

Based purely on expected value theory, the council should buy a new snow plough since they could save $1,000 more than the machine costs.

39 Expected value selling ice cream

= (0.6 × –$50) + 0.4 × ($150) = –$30 + $60 = $30

Expected value selling umbrellas

= (0.6 × $200) + (0.4 × –$10) = $120 + ($4) = $116

so choose umbrellas.

40 (i) Expected profit from new product is

(0.1 × $100,000) + (0.5 × $50,000) + (0.4 × –20,000)

= $10,000 + $25,000 – $8,000

= $27,000

(ii) $27,000

PAPER C03 : FUNDAMENTALS OF BUSINESS MATHEMATICS

41 A (i) It is an objective way of making investment decisions.

   (ii) Over the long term, the correct decision will be taken.

   B (i) On individual projects the wrong decision may be made because of random events.

   (ii) A 10% chance of winning $1,000 would show a higher expected value than a 90% chance of winning $100 but would it be the correct decision to take?

42 Project A = (0.5 × $5,000) + (0.5 × $2,500)

   = $3,750

   Project B = (0.3 × $10,000) + (0.7 × $1,000)

   = $3,700

   Project C = (0.4 × $6,000) + (0.6 × $4,000)

   = $4,800

   So 1C, 2A, 3B

43 CIGARETTE SALES PROMOTION

The average value of a prize is calculated as follows

Value (x) $	Frequency f	fx
0.20	5	1.00
0.50	2	1.00
1.00	1	1.00
	8	3.00

Mean = $\dfrac{\Sigma fx}{\Sigma f} = \dfrac{3.00}{8} = 37.5\text{p}$

Total cost = Average cost per leaflet × no. of leaflets

$75,000 = 0.375 × x

$x = \dfrac{£75,000}{0.375} = 200,000$

So 200,000 leaflets should be used.

44 (i) Probability that first number uncovered is not a winner = $\dfrac{30}{37}$

   This would leave 36 numbers and 29 non-winners.

   Probability that the second number is not a winner = $\dfrac{29}{36}$

   This would leave 35 numbers and 28 non-winners.

   Similarly for all 7 numbers, hence

   P (no win) = $\dfrac{30}{37} \times \dfrac{29}{36} \times \dfrac{28}{35} \times \dfrac{27}{34} \times \dfrac{26}{33} \times \dfrac{25}{32} \times \dfrac{24}{31}$

   = 0.1977

(ii) Probability that first number uncovered is a winner = $\frac{7}{37}$

This would leave 36 numbers and 6 winners.

Probability that the second number is a winner = $\frac{6}{36}$ etc.

Hence

$$P \text{ (all win)} = \frac{7}{37} \times \frac{6}{36} \times \frac{5}{35} \times \frac{4}{34} \times \frac{3}{33} \times \frac{2}{32} \times \frac{1}{31}$$

$$= 0.189 \times 0.167 \times 0.143 \times 0.118 \times 0.091 \times 0.063 \times 0.032$$

$$= 9.771 \times 10^{-8}$$

The expected number of Super Prizes in 1 million cards is $9.713 \times 10^{-8} \times 106$ (i.e. probability × no. of cards: $9.771 \times 10^{-8} \times 10^6 = 0.09771$

This is the probability that the Super Prizes is won in one promotion.

The chance is, therefore 1 in $\frac{1}{0.09771}$

= 1 in 10 (approximately)

45 Contribution per programme sold is (60p — 10p) = 50p. The table shows expected profits (needed for part (b)) found by working 4.

Demand			Production		
(probability in brackets)	1,000	2,000	3,000	4,000	5,000
1,000 (0.1)	(W1) $0	(W2) $(100)	$(200)	$(300)	$(400)
2,000 (0.4)	$0	(W3) $500	$400	$300	$200
3,000 (0.2)	$0	$500	$1,000	$900	$800
4,000 (0.2)	$0	$500	$1,000	$1,500	$1,400
5,000 (0.1)	$0	$500	$1,000	$1,500	$2,000
Expected $ value	$0	(W4) $440	$640	$720	$680

Workings

(W1) Contribution from sales of 1,000 = 500
Less: (Fixed print cost — Advertising revenue) = (500)

nil

(W2) Contribution from sales of 1,000 = 500
Less (500)
Less: 1,000 programmes printed and sold @ $0.10 = (100)

(100)

(W3) Contribution from sales of 2,000 = 1,000
Less (500)

500

(W4) $(0.1 \times 100) + (0.4 \times 500) + (0.2 \times 500) + (0.2 \times 500) + (0.1 \times 500) = \$440$.

SUMMARISING AND ANALYSING DATA

PRESENTATION OF DATA

46 Principles to be followed constructing graphs and diagrams
- (i) give the diagram a name
- (ii) state where data is sourced
- (iii) units of measurement must be stated
- (iv) scale must be stated
- (v) axes must be clearly labelled
- (vi) neatness is essential

47
- (i) simple
- (ii) component
- (iii) multiple

48
- (i) wheat $\frac{43}{100} \times 360$ 155°
- (ii) barley $\frac{20}{100} \times 360$ 72°
- (iii) grass $\frac{16}{100} \times 360$ 58°
- (iv) oats $\frac{12}{100} \times 360$ 43°
- (v) fallow $\frac{9}{100} \times 360$ 32°

49

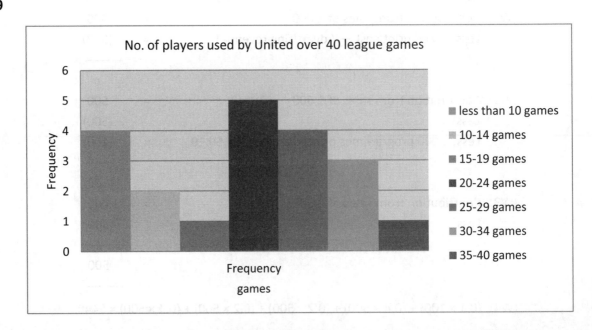

50

Class interval Weight	Frequency No of articles	Cumulative Frequency
100 and less than 110	1	1
110 and less than 120	2	3
120 and less than 130	5	8
130 and less than 140	11	19
140 and less than 150	21	40
150 and less than 160	20	60
160 and less than 170	17	77
170 and less than 180	11	88
180 and less than 190	6	94
190 and less than 200	6	100

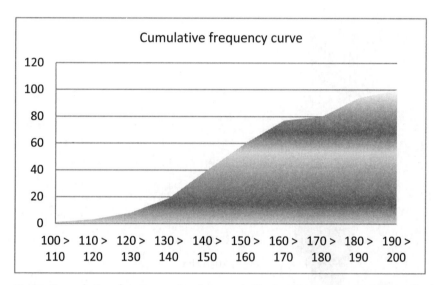

Note: Cumulative frequency is always plotted at the upper mathematical class limit.

51

(i) Pie chart

	2001		2002	
	Sales	Angles	Sales	Angles
UK	31.5	86.5°	35.0	70.2°
EC	33.2	91.2°	47.4	95.1°
USA	40.3	110.7°	78.9	158.2°
Australia	26.1	71.6°	18.2	36.5°
	131.1	360.0°	179.5	360.0°

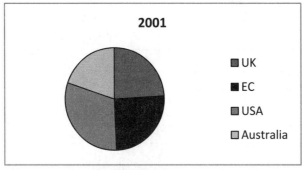

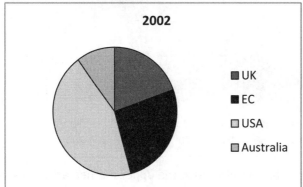

(ii)

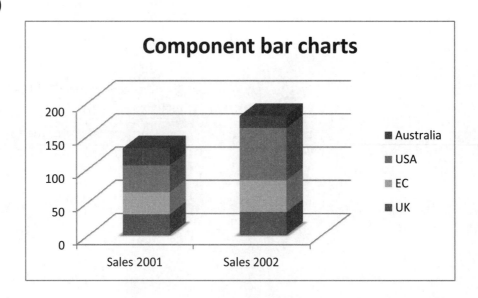

ANSWERS TO PRACTICE QUESTIONS : SECTION 3

52

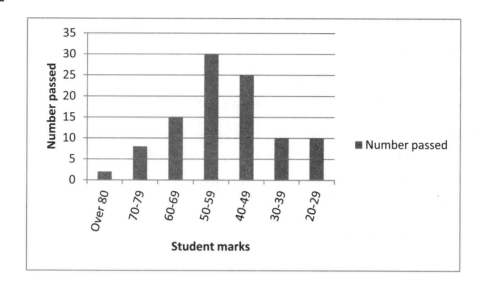

53

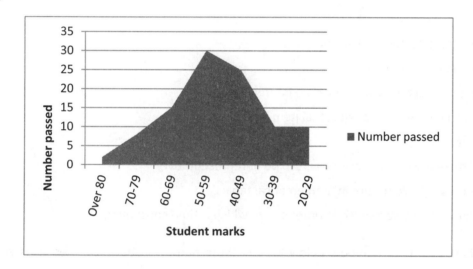

AVERAGES

54 (i) The *arithmetic mean* is calculated by taking the total value of all items divided by the total number of items.

(ii) The *median* is the value of the middle item in a distribution once all the items have been arranged in order of magnitude.

(iii) The *mode* is the value that occurs most frequently amongst all the items in the distribution.

55 THE MEAN

Advantages

(i) Easy to calculate and understand.

(ii) All the data in the distribution is used.

(iii) It can be used in more advanced mathematical statistics.

Disadvantages

(i) It may give undue weight or be influenced by extreme values e.g. income

(ii) The value of the average may not correspond to any individual value in the distribution for example 2.2 children.

56 $$\frac{3+6+7+8+9+11+13+15}{8} = \frac{72}{8} = 9$$

57 THE MEDIAN

Advantages

(i) It is not affected by extreme values.

(ii) It is easy to understand.

(iii) It is unaffected by unequal class intervals.

(iv) It can be the value of an actual item in the distribution.

Disadvantages

(i) If there are only a few items it can be unrepresentative.

(ii) It is unsuitable for use in mathematical tables.

(iii) Data has to be arranged in order of size which is time consuming.

58 Since there are three numbers below 14 and three numbers above 14, median is equal to 14.

59 THE MODE

Advantages

(i) It is easy to understand and calculate,

(ii) It is not affected by extreme values.

(iii) It can be calculated even if all the values in the distribution are not known.

(iv) It can be the value of an item in the distribution.

Disadvantages

(i) There may be no modal value or more than one may exist.

(ii) It is not suitable for mathematical statistics.

(iii) Data has to be arranged to ascertain which figure appears the most often.

60 The modal value is four since it appears three times.

ANSWERS TO PRACTICE QUESTIONS : SECTION 3

61 GOLFER'S SCORE

(i) Mean $= \dfrac{67 + 71 + 72 + 73 + 72 + 69 + 71 + 72}{8}$

$= 71$

(ii) Median = 67, 69, 71, 71, 72, 72, 72, 73

In this example the median is found by taking the arithmetic mean of 71 and 72 so 71.5

(iii) The score which appears the most frequently is 72.

62 ESTIMATION OF MODE FOR GROUPED DATA

In a grouped frequency distribution, the modal class is the class with the largest frequency. This can easily be found by observation. The value of the mode within the modal class can then be estimated from a histogram.

Having located the modal class it is necessary to draw in the dotted lines shown in the following diagram.

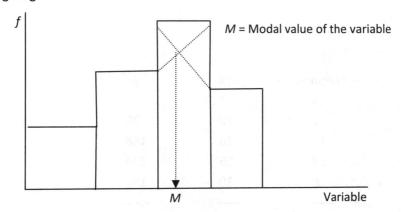

63

Class interval	Mid-value	Frequency	
Weight (grams)	x	f	fx
100 and less than 110	105	1	105
110 and less than 120	115	2	230
120 and less than 130	125	5	625
130 and less than 140	135	11	1,485
140 and less than 150	145	21	3,045
150 and less than 160	155	20	3,100
160 and less than 170	165	17	2,805
170 and less than 180	175	11	1,925
180 and less than 190	185	6	1,110
190 and less than 200	195	6	1,170

$\overline{X} = \dfrac{\Sigma fx}{\Sigma f} = \dfrac{15,600}{100} = 156g$

PAPER C03 : FUNDAMENTALS OF BUSINESS MATHEMATICS

VARIATION

64

x	x^2
3	9
4	16
6	36
8	64
9	81
30	206

$$\sigma = \sqrt{\frac{206}{5} - \left(\frac{30}{5}\right)^2}$$

$$= \sqrt{41.2 - 36}$$

$$= \sqrt{5.2}$$

$$= 2.28$$

65

x	Frequency	fx	fx^2
1	3	3	3
2	5	10	20
3	12	36	108
4	14	56	224
5	6	30	150
Total	40	135	505

$$\sigma = \sqrt{\frac{505}{40} - \left(\frac{135}{40}\right)^2}$$

$$= \sqrt{12.63 - 11.39}$$

$$= \sqrt{1.24}$$

$$= 1.11$$

66 Product A coefficient of variation = $\dfrac{1.29 \times 100}{5.46} = 23.63\%$

Product B coefficient of variation = $\dfrac{4.21 \times 100}{16.38} = 25.7\%$

67

x	x^2
8,000	64×10^6
7,500	56.25×10^6
8,200	67.24×10^6
9,100	82.81×10^6
8,500	72.25×10^6
8,400	70.56×10^6
6,200	38.44×10^6
8,100	65.61×10^6
8,200	67.24×10^6
8,100	65.61×10^6
8,400	70.56×10^6
10,000	100×10^6
98,700	820,570,000
10,000	100×10^6
98,700	820.57×10^6

or

$$\sigma = \sqrt{\frac{820.57 \times 10^6}{12} - \left(\frac{98,700}{12}\right)^2}$$

$$= \sqrt{68.38 \times 10^6 - 67.65 \times 10^6}$$

$$= \sqrt{0.73 \times 10^6}$$

$$= 854.4$$

68

Time	Tally	Frequency
105 > 110	II	2
110 > 115		5
115 > 120	IIII	4
120 > 125	III	8
125 > 130		10
130 > 135		5
135 > 140	IIII	4
140 > 145	II	2

69 By constructing cumulative frequency distribution

(i) median = 126 seconds

70

Time	Mid-point	f	fx	fx²
105–110	107.5	2	215	23,112.50
110–115	112.5	5	562.5	63,281.25
115–120	117.5	4	470	55,225.00
120–125	122.5	8	980	120,050.00
125–130	127.5	10	1,275	162,562.50
130–135	132.5	5	662.5	87,781.25
135–140	137.5	4	550	75,625.00
140–145	142.5	2	285	40,612.50
		$\Sigma f = 40$	$\Sigma fx = 5,000$	$\Sigma fx^2 = 628,250.00$

$$\text{Mean} = \frac{\Sigma fx}{\Sigma f} = \frac{5,000}{40} = 125 \text{ seconds}$$

71 Standard deviation $= \sqrt{\dfrac{628,250}{40} - \left(\dfrac{5,000}{40}\right)^2}$

$= 9.01\%$

THE NORMAL DISTRIBUTION

72 (i) It is symmetrical and bell shaped.

(ii) Both tails approach but never reach the X axis.

(iii) The mean, median and mode are equal.

(iv) The area under the curve is equal to 1 and the areas left and right of the mean are equal to 0.5 each.

(v) It is a mathematical curve which closely fits many natural occurring distributions.

73 (i) heights of people

(ii) weights of people

(iii) examination marks

ANSWERS TO PRACTICE QUESTIONS : SECTION 3

74 (i) $\dfrac{430 - 400}{60} = 0.5$

From table 0.5 − 0.1915 = 0.3085 or approximately 31%

(ii) $\dfrac{350 - 400}{60} = -0.83$

From table 0.5 − 0.2967 = 0.2033 or approximately 20%.

(iii) $\dfrac{460 - 400}{60} = 1$

From table 0.5 − 0.3413 = 0.1587 or approximately 16%.

(iv) Area less than $350 has already been found in (ii) = 0.2033

therefore area between $350 and $400 = 0.5 − 0.2033 = 0.2967

similarly area over $430 has already been found in (i) = 0.3085

therefore area between $400 and $430 = 0.5 − 0.3085 = 0.1915

therefore area between $350 and $430 = 0.2967 + 0.1915 = 0.4882

so approximately 49% earn between $350 and $430.

(v) If area over $430 is 0.3085 then area between $400 and $430 is 0.5 − 0.3085 = 0.1915

If area over $460 is 0.1587 then area between $400 and $460 is 0.5 − 0.1587 = 0.3413

so area between $430 and $460 = 0.3413 − 0.1915 = 0.1498

so approximately 15% earn between $430 and $460.

75 A (i) $Z = \dfrac{x - v}{\sigma} = \dfrac{60 - 70}{5} = -\dfrac{10}{5} = -2$

from tables 0.02275

Thus the chance of temperature being below 60° is 2.2%.

(ii) $Z = \dfrac{65 - 70}{5} = -1$

from tables probability of temperature less than 65° is 0.1587.

So probability that temperature is no lower than 65%

= 1 − 0.1587 = 0.8413

So there is an 84% chance temperature is no lower than 65°.

(iii) $Z = \dfrac{85 - 70}{5} = 3$

Thus the probability of temperature higher than 85° is 0.13%

B Since most normal distribution tables only go up to 2.99

we cannot find value of 3.

However, taking a guess it would be about 1%.

76 $u = 50$

$\sigma = 10$

$n = 100$

$x = 48$

Standard error $= \dfrac{\sigma}{n} = \dfrac{10}{100} = 0.1$

$Z = \dfrac{48 - 50}{1} = -2$

from table area = 0.2275 = 0.5 – 0.4772 – 0.0228

that is 48 is Z standard errors below mean weight of 50

so probability = 2.3%.

INTERRELATIONSHIP BETWEEN VARIABLES

CORRELATION AND REGRESSION

77

X	Y	XY	X^2
25	124	3,100	625
22	131	2,882	484
16	98	1,568	256
12	74	888	144
7	56	392	49
8	65	520	64
15	114	1,710	225
12	86	1,032	144
$\Sigma X = 117$	$\Sigma Y = 748$	$\Sigma XY = 12,092$	$\Sigma X^2 = 1,991$

$Y = a + bx$ where a = fixed costs and b = variable costs

$b = \dfrac{(8 \times 12,092) - (117 \times 748)}{(8 \times 1,991) - (117 \times 117)}$ formula: $\dfrac{n\Sigma XY - (\Sigma X \bullet \Sigma Y)}{n\Sigma X^2 - \Sigma X \bullet \Sigma X}$

$= \dfrac{96,736 - 87,516}{15,928 - 13,689} = \dfrac{9,220}{2,239} = 4.12$

$a = 93.50 - 14.625 \times 4.12 = 935.50 - 60.26 = \$33.24$

Fixed cost = $33.24 and variable cost = $4.12

78   A value of 0.87 indicates a high degree of positive correlation between hours used and power costs. This tells us that 87% of the variation in power costs can be attributed to changes in the hours used and 13% on other factors. However, a sample of eight is quite small. Nevertheless, +0.87 is close to +1 which indicates a perfect positive relationship.

79 and 80

X	Y	XY	X^2
1	40	40	1
2	45	90	4
3	50	150	9
4	65	260	16
5	70	350	25
6	70	420	36
7	80	560	49
28	420	1,870	140

79 $b = \dfrac{(7 \times 1,870) - (28 \times 420)}{(7 \times 140) - (28 \times 28)}$

$= \dfrac{13,090 - 11,760}{980 - 784} = 6.79$

$a = \dfrac{420}{7} - 6.79 \times \dfrac{28}{7}$

$= 60 - 27.16 = 32.84$

Regression line for y on x = $y = 32.84 + 6.79x$

80 $\dfrac{7 \times 1,870 - (28 \times 420)}{\sqrt{(7 \times 140 - (28 \times 28))(7 \times 26,550 - 420^2)}}$

$= \dfrac{13,090 - 11,760}{\sqrt{(980 - 784)(185,850 - 176,400)}}$

$= \dfrac{1,330}{\sqrt{196 \times 9,450}}$

$= 0.98$

PAPER C03 : FUNDAMENTALS OF BUSINESS MATHEMATICS

81

(i)

Student	Maths test	English test	D	D^2
A	4	2	2	4
B	5	3	2	4
C	2	1	1	1
D	1	4	−3	9
E	3	5	−2	4
F	6	6	0	0
			ΣD_0	ΣD^2

$$r = 1 - \frac{6 \times 22}{6 \times (6^2 - 1)}$$

$$= 1 - \frac{132}{210}$$

$$= \frac{78}{210}$$

$$= 0.37$$

(ii) (c)

82 (i) +1

(ii) −1

(iii) 0

83 $1,000 + 5,000 (7.5 g)

= $1,000 + $37,500

= $38,500

84 $y = 20 - 0.25x$

If $x = 12$ $y = 20 - 0.25 \times 12$

$y = 20 - 3$

$y = 17\%$

ANSWERS TO PRACTICE QUESTIONS : SECTION 3

85 Σx^2 = 12,614

      Σx = 320

      Σy = 130

      n = 10

      Σxy = 4,728

$$b = \frac{10 \times 4{,}728 - (320 \times 130)}{10 \times 12{,}614 - 320^2}$$

$$= \frac{5{,}680}{23{,}740}$$

$$= 0.239$$

$$a = \frac{130 - 0.239 \times 320}{10}$$

$$= 5.34$$

Least squares regression is $y = 5.34 + 0.239x$

86 $5.34 + 0.239 \times 15 = 8.93$ so $8,930

      $5.34 + 0.239 \times 55 = 18.5$ so $18,500

FORECASTING

TIME SERIES

87   Quarter 4 = $\dfrac{145}{133} \times 100 = 109$ same as Quarter 1

88   (i)   change in population

       (ii)   down turn in economic activity

       (iii)   rise in goods sold before Christmas

       (iv)   events in New York September 11th 2001

89   A = actual value for the period

      T = trend component

      C = cyclical component

      S = seasonal component

      R = residual component

90

1st quarter	=	13
		22
		58
		23
		───
		116 ÷ 4 = 29
2nd quarter	=	22
		58
		23
		16
		───
		119 ÷ 4 = 29.75 ≈ 30

So 29, 30, 31, 32, 33, 33, 33, 33, 33, 34, 34, 35, 36

91 Trend equals central value of four quarterly moving average

So 1st trend = (29 + 29.75)/2

2nd trend = (29.75 + 31.25)/2

So rounded up 29, 31, 32, 32, 33, 33, 33, 33, 33, 34, 34, 35

92

Quarter 1	−16
Quarter 2	−5
Quarter 3	28
Quarter 4	−8

93

19 − (−16)	35
32 − (−5)	37
65 − 29	37 (T = Y − S)
30 − (−8)	38

Yes, upward trend has continued

94 Forecast = T × S

Sales last quarter 240 Q^2

Seasonally for Q^2 = +50   ∴ S = 150

Trend = $\dfrac{240}{150\%} = \dfrac{240}{1.5} = 160$

Seasonality = −50%   ∴ S = 50%

Forecast = 160 × 50% = 160 × 0.5 = 80

ANSWERS TO PRACTICE QUESTIONS : SECTION 3

95 $y = 345 - 1.5x$

$x = 19$ so $y = 345 - 28.5 = 316.5$

Seasonally adjusted $316.5 - 23.5 = 293$

96 $y = 7.5 + 3.8x$

Seasonal variation $= 1.12 \times$ trend

For month 16, $y = (7.5 + 3.8 \times 16)\, 1.12 = (7.5 + 60.8)\, 1.12 = 68.3 \times 1.12$

$Y = 76.5$

FINANCIAL MATHEMATICS

97

Year	Investment $
1	100
2	200
3	300
4	400
5	500

So $500

98

Year	Principal $	Interest $	Total $
1	100	10	110
2	110	11	121
3	121	12.10	133.10
4	133.10	13.31	146.41
5	146.41	14.64	161.05

99 $x = \$5,000$

$r = 8\% = \dfrac{8}{100} = 0.08\quad n = 5$

$D = x(1-r)^n = \$5,000 \times (1 - 0.08)^5 = \$5,000 \times 0.6591$

$= \$3,295$

PAPER C03 : FUNDAMENTALS OF BUSINESS MATHEMATICS

100 $D = \$100 \quad x = \$8,000 \quad n = 10$

so $100 = 8,000 (1 - r)^{10}$

$(1 - r)^{10} = \dfrac{100}{8,000} = 0.0125$

$(1 - r) = 0.0125^{1/10}$

$= 0.6452$

$r = 1 - 0.6452 = 0.3548 = 35.48\%$

101 Assume first instalment is paid immediately

$S_n = \dfrac{A(R^n - 1)}{R - 1}$ where A = annual savings R = 1.09 n = 6

S_n is the amount saved after 6 years

$= \dfrac{\$400 \times (1.09^6 - 1)}{1.09 - 1}$ Yes, he will save enough money in 5 years time.

$= \$3,009$

102 See annuity table. Check values of 6% at year 14 and year 4

PV $= \$5,000$ (year 14 – year 4)

$= \$5,000 (9.295 - 3.465)$

$= \$29,150$

103 Again go straight to cumulative present value and look up the value for 9% at eight years = 5.535

So $\dfrac{£50,000}{5.535} = \$9,033.42$ per annum

104 Present value of perpetuity is $\$10,000 \times \dfrac{1}{0.05} = \$200,000$.

105 NET PRESENT VALUE

Year	Cash flow $	DCF–12%	Present value
0	(2,000)	1	(2,000)
1	500	0.893	447
2	500	0.797	399
3	600	0.712	427
4	600	0.636	382
5	440	0.567	249

Net present value – $96

Internal rate of return 8%

Year	Cash flow $	DCF-8%	Present value
0	(2,000)	1	(2,000)
1	500	0.926	463
2	500	0.857	429
3	600	0.794	476
4	600	0.735	441
5	440	0.681	300

Net present value = $109

IRR is between 12% and 8%

So IRR $= A + \left(\dfrac{NA}{NA - NB}\right) \times B - A$

$= 8\% + \left(\dfrac{109}{109 - (-96)}\right) \times (12\% - 8\%)$

$= 8\% + \left(\dfrac{109}{205}\right) \times 4\% = 10.13\%$

Reject NPV because at 12% it is negative.

Reject IRR because it is below 12%.

106

$(1 + r)^{12} = 1.30$

There are 12 months in a year

So $1 + r = \sqrt[12]{1.3} = 2.21$

So r = 2.21%

PAPER C03 : FUNDAMENTALS OF BUSINESS MATHEMATICS

SPREADSHEETS

107 The answer is

=ROUND(MEDIAN(A2:D7),1)

Working

The ROUND function that encircles the basic MEDIAN function is there to set the number of decimal places – here to just one place. Remember that formatting the cell will only change the displayed number of decimal places not the actual value held.

If the mode were required rather than the median, the formula would become =ROUND(MODE(A2:D7),1)

108 The answer is

=$B$1*(1+$B$2)^B4

Working

The references to the cells containing the amount invested and the interest rate must be fixed to prevent them being altered as the formula is copied.

109 The NPV would be calculated as

= NPV(B7,B2:B5)+B1

Working

The investment figure has been entered into the spreadsheet as a negative figure here and must therefore be added to the discounted cash flows.

The IRR would be

=IRR(B1:B5)

Working

NB If the calculation did not work, resulting in the answer #NUM!, it would be necessary to add an alternative guess to the 10% used as a default such as 20%, that is =IRR(Bl:B5,0.2)

110 (i) =ROUND(38/3*42.3^2,3)

(ii) =ROUND(SQRT(220)*4^2,0)

NB: Alternatively you can also set 220 to the power of a half: =ROUND(220^(1/2)*4^2,0)

111 The answer is

=FORECAST(A2,$B$2:$B$7,$A$2:$A$7)

Working

Note that the first cell is not fixed as that will need to alter to reflect the actual level of rainfall in each row. However the cells marking the range of findings against which it is plotted are fixed.

ANSWERS TO PRACTICE QUESTIONS : SECTION 3

112 (i) Build in cross-checks to validate data/calculations

(ii) Keep the use absolute values in formulae to a minimum

(iii) Keep graphs on separate chart sheets where possible

(iv) Use colour coded fonts on larger plans

(v) Ensure the worksheets are labelled and dated.

113 (i) Worksheets are described using column letters and row numbers. Each row/column co-ordinate is referred to as a cell and each cell has a unique address. For example, the cell where column C and row 8 intersect is referred to as cell C8. Cell references are used in the creation of formulae.

(ii) An Excel file is called a workbook. A workbook can consist of a single worksheet or a combination of multiple worksheets, charts, databases and so on.

(iii) A worksheet is a grid of rows and columns, forming a series of cells. Most of the work done in Excel will be done on worksheets.

(iv) Macros are the record of a series of keystrokes or mouse clicks.

114 Formatting a cell changes the display so that only 2 decimal places are viewed. It is important to remember that cells that are formatted still hold the data as before and if calculations are performed on them will use the pure number not the one on display. The =ROUND function must be used to actually round the data held in the cell. Calculations performed on the data will then use the rounded figure.

115 A template is a plan that contains the logic required for the plan to work but with all the data removed. When new data is entered then the plan is created.

Advantages include:

- Business plans take time to design and create. The template stores this effort for future use.
- Using a template ensures that plans made at different times or for different departments are directly comparable.
- Preparing the template will help identify any inappropriate use of absolute values which can be rectified for future use.
- New plans can be drawn up far more quickly.

116 Excel can perform over 350 functions. Some of those that have been covered in the syllabus include:

- Plotting graphs of equations
- Drawing graphs (histograms, ogives, pie charts) to present data
- Calculation of statistical functions such as standard deviation and variance
- Calculation of NPV and IRR
- Drawing scatter diagrams
- Plotting the line of least squares
- 'What-if?' analysis.

117 First a scatter diagram needs to be created using the data gathered.

This is done by selecting the range containing the data (here B2:C7), and using the chart icon to select an XY scatter chart

Next, a least squares column is needed.

For this, we need to identify the independent variable - here the data in column B, and then set up the forecast function. The range is fixed using $ signs, and linked to each independent variable in turn. Note that the dependent variables are specified before the dependent ones when the range is given:

	A	B	C	D
1	Region	Advertising spend $(000s)	Sales revenue $(000s)	Least squared line
2	North West	12.5	31.25	= FORECAST(B2,$C$2:$C$7,$B$2:$B$7)
3	North East	14.3	30.03	= FORECAST(B3,$C$2:$C$7,$B$2:$B$7)
4	Midlands	16.7	37.91	= FORECAST(B4,$C$2:$C$7,$B$2:$B$7)
5	South East	14.4	33.12	= FORECAST(B5,$C$2:$C$7,$B$2:$B$7)
6	South West	11.7	24.57	= FORECAST(B6,$C$2:$C$7,$B$2:$B$7)
7	London	13.5	25.52	= FORECAST(B7,$C$2:$C$7,$B$2:$B$7)

The least squares column (D2:D7) can now be copied onto the chart.

Finally, by selecting one of the data symbols and setting Line to Automatic, the line is revealed.

118 (a) The benefits to the Scout Group of using Excel:
- Avoids the need for manual calculations – quicker and more accurate
- By using calculation cross-checks, any missing data can be quickly identified
- Once individual budgets have been drawn up (probably on separate worksheets within a workbook), they can be simply combined into an annual group budget.
- 'What-if' analysis can be performed. For example, the impact of additional children joining, or a lower than expected amount raised from a fund-raising event, can be simply analysed.
- If leaders need to explain any assumptions they have made, they can be simply included by means of a 'Comment' inserted into a cell.
- The budgets drawn up this year will provide a working template to reduce work significantly in future years.

(b) How the budgets can be drawn up to reduce the workload:
- It would be worth agreeing a common format for each section, to simplify the process of drawing together the information into a group budget.
- To avoid confusion, the rows and columns should be clearly labelled and colour coded as necessary
- All absolute values should be kept in a separate data table away from the main part of the budget. The budget should then be created using formula, which use the data in the table as needed. This will ensure that the impact of any changes to the estimates when put through into the data table will immediately flow through into the budget.
- Once the budget for the year has been created, a copy should be made. The data in the table is removed and the cells containing the formula protected. This Template can then be used to draw up future year's budgets more quickly.
- To avoid minor mathematical variations due to rounding, the formula should be set to round to two decimal places. Note that it is not enough to format the cells, since this changes the display but not the underlying value held.

119

Time	Cash flow	DF @ 10%	PV @ 10%	DF @ 20%	PV @ 20%
T_0	(50,000)	1	(50,000)	1	(50,000)
T_1	12,000	0.909	10,908	0.833	9,996
T_2	15,000	0.826	12,390	0.694	10,410
T_3	14,000	0.751	10,514	0.597	8,358
T_4	22,000	0.683	15,026	0.482	10,604
T_5	18,000	0.621	11,178	0.402	7,236
	Total NPV		10,016		(3,396)

The NPV at 10% is $10,016 and the investment should be accepted.

$$IRR = R1 + \left[(R_2 - R_1) \times \frac{NPV_1}{NPV_1 - NPV_2}\right]$$

$$IRR = 10 + \left[(20 - 10) \times \frac{10,016}{10,016 - (3,396)}\right]$$

$$IRR = 10 + \left[10 \times \frac{10,016}{13,412}\right]$$

$IRR = 10 + [10 \times 0.7467]$

$IRR = 10 + 7.47 = 17.5\%$

The IRR is above the cost of capital of 10% which also leads to the conclusion that the project should be accepted.

Obviously the cash flows can be entered into any column of cells. The purpose here is to clarify the range that is being included in the NPV and IRR formulae.

	A	B
1		
2	Time	Cash flows
3	T_0	−50000
4	T_1	12000
5	T_2	15000
6	T_3	14000
7	T_4	22000
8	T_5	18000
9		
10	Cost of capital	10%
11	NPV =	= NPV(B10,B4:B8) + B3
12	IRR =	= IRR(B3:B8)

Section 4

ANSWERS TO OBJECTIVE TEST QUESTIONS

BASIC MATHEMATICS

FORMULAE

1   D

$6a + 6b + 2a - 3b$ is equal to $8a + 3b$.

2   A

We need to multiply the numbers and add the powers so $3a^3 + 4a^4 = 12a^7$.

3   D

$$8^{-2} = \frac{1}{8^2} = \frac{1}{64}$$

4   D

$$35^{-0.5} = \frac{1}{\sqrt{36}} = \frac{1}{6}$$

5   A

Statement A is incorrect since Z is less than both X and Y.

6   C

$4 + 3 - 2 \times (8 - 3) = 4 + 3 - 2 \times 5 = 4 + 3 - 10 = -3$

7   B

If $X \leq Y$, this implies that X is less than or equal to Y.

PAPER C03: FUNDAMENTALS OF BUSINESS MATHEMATICS

8 A

$$\frac{2}{7}+\frac{3}{8}=\frac{16}{56}+\frac{21}{56}=\frac{37}{56}$$

Note: 2/7 multiplied by 8 to get LCD

3/8 multiplied by 7 to get LCD

9 C

A similar question to Q2, top equation becomes x^9, so $\frac{x^9}{x^7}=x^2$

10 A

Addition and multiplication do not affect the order in which the numbers appear.

PERCENTAGES, RATIOS AND PROPORTIONS

11 D

If cost price = 100%

then selling price is 120% of cost

120% of cost = $240

100% of cost = $240 \times \frac{100}{120}$

= $200

Profit = $240 − $200 = $40

12 D

Gross profit = $\frac{£200}{£500}$ = 40%

13 C

Total profit to be distributed = $36,000

Alex receives $\frac{7}{18} \times \$36{,}000 = \$14{,}000$

14 B

$\frac{54{,}000}{278{,}000} = \frac{27}{139} = 19\%$

15 B

Ex VAT price = $\frac{£298}{117.5} \times 100 = \$253.62$

ANSWERS TO OBJECTIVE TEST QUESTIONS : SECTION 4

16 D

x% of 200 = 200 × (x/100) = 2x

17 D

We can eliminate A and B since they only go to one decimal place. At three decimal places 0.379 is closer to 0.38 than 0.37.

18 C

		Depreciation	
Value year 1	9,000	3,000	12,000 × 0.25
Value year 2	6,750	2,250	9,000 × 0.25
Value year 3	5,062.50	1,687.50	6,750 × 0.25

19 C

No. of managers = 10

No. of seniors = $\dfrac{15 \times 14}{2 \times 1} = 105$

No. of assistants = $\dfrac{20 \times 19 \times 18 \times 17}{4 \times 3 \times 2 \times 1} = 4{,}845$

Therefore number of different audit teams = 10 × 105 × 4,845

= 5,087,250

20 C

1st game		2nd game	
City	United	City	United
won	lost	Lost	won
won	lost	Won	lost
won	lost	Draw	draw
draw	draw	Lost	won
draw	draw	Won	lost
draw	draw	Draw	draw
lost	won	Lost	won
lost	won	Won	lost
lost	won	draw	draw

= 9

PAPER C03 : FUNDAMENTALS OF BUSINESS MATHEMATICS

ACCURACY AND ROUNDING

21 D

$$\frac{£117.58 - £105.26}{£117.58} \times 100 = 10.48\%$$

22 C

The percentage increase over the two years is (167 − 115)/115 = 45.22%

Average annual increase = $\sqrt{1.4522} - 1 = 0.2051 = 20.51\%$

23 A

85/1.175 = 72.34 (excluding VAT)

72.34 × 1.15 = 83.19 (with 15% VAT)

EQUATIONS AND GRAPHS

24 B

Volume of rectangular box is equal to length × height × depth.

1,458 = 2x × x × x

1,458 = 2x³

729 = x³

$\sqrt[3]{729} = x$

x = 9

25 A

Total cost = Fixed cost + Variable cost
= $10,000 + $7.5x

26 C

x = a + bp since graph of this function is linear

when x = 400 p = 40

400 = a + 40b   (1)

when x = 800 p = 20

800 = a + 20b   (2)

subtracting (1) from (2)

we have 400 = −20b

$\frac{400}{-20} = b$

so $b = -20$

using equation (1)

$400 = a + 40 \times (-20)$

$400 = a - 800$

$400 + 800 = a$

$a = 1,200$

so $x = 1,200 - 20p$

$20p = 1,200 - x$

$p = \dfrac{1,200 - x}{20} = 60 - \dfrac{x}{20}$

Sales revenue = $x \times p$

so $x \times \left(60 - \dfrac{x}{20}\right)$

27 A

The profit equation is total revenue – total cost

$= \left(60x - \dfrac{x^2}{20}\right) - (10,000 + 7.5x)$

$= \dfrac{-x^2}{20} + 52.5x - 10,000$

28 B

$3x + 4y = 25$ (1)

$10x + 2y = 38$ (2)

Multiply equation (2) by 2

$20x + 4y = 76$

$3x + 4y = 25$

$17x = 51$

$x = 3$

$3x + 4y = 25$

$9 + 4y = 25$

$4y = 16$

$y = 4$

so $x = 3$ and $y — 4$

PAPER C03 : FUNDAMENTALS OF BUSINESS MATHEMATICS

29 C

Using the formula

$$x = \frac{-b \pm \sqrt{b^2 - 4ac}}{2a}$$

where a = 9   b = –30   c = 25

$$x = \frac{-(-30) \pm \sqrt{900 - 900}}{18}$$

$$= \frac{30 \pm 0}{18}$$

$$= \frac{5}{3}$$

30 B

The shape of a graph of a linear equation will be a straight line.

31 B

If $b^2 - 4ac$ is zero, there is only one solution

If $b^2 - 4ac$ is positive, there are two solutions

If $b^2 - 4ac$ is negative, there are no solutions

32 A

Eliminate x (either of the other variables would do) between (1) and (2):

3 × (1): 6x + 9y + 12z = 27

2 × (2): 6x – 4y – 6z = 6

Subtract: 13y + 18z = 21   (4)

Eliminate x between (3) and (1), ((2) could have been used instead of (1)):

2 × (1): 4x + 6y + 8z = 18

(3): 4x + 5y – 2z = 25

Subtract: y + 10z = –7   (5)

Multiply equation (5) by 13

13y + 130z = –91   (6)

Subtract (4) from (6)

13y + 130z = –91   (6)

13y + 18z = 21   (4)

112z = –112

ANSWERS TO OBJECTIVE TEST QUESTIONS : SECTION 4

Rearrange the equation to obtain a value for z.

$112z = -112$

$z = \dfrac{-112}{112}$

$z = -1$

Substitute the value of z into equation (5)

$y + 10z = -7$

$y + 10(-l) = -7$

$y - 10 = -7$

$y = -7 + 10$

$y = 3$

Due to there being three unknowns, substitute the values for y and z into equation (1) to obtain a value for x.

$2x + 3y + 4z = 9$ (1)

$2x + 3 \times (3) + 4 \times (-1) = 9$

$2x + 9 - 4 = 9$

$2x = 9 - 9 + 4$

$2x = 4$

$x = \dfrac{4}{2}$

$x = 2$

Check in either (2) or (3):

From (2): $3 \times 2 - 2 \times 3 - 3 \times (-1) = 3$

$6 - 6 + 3 = 3$

$3 = 3$

Hence the solution is $x = 2, y = 3, z = -1$

33 A

$6x^2 + 12x = 4(5x + 2)$

$6x^2 + 12x = 20x + 8$

$6x^2 - 8x - 8 = 0$

$x = \dfrac{-(-8) \pm \sqrt{(-8)^2 - (4 \times 6 \times (-8))}}{2 \times 6}$

$= \dfrac{8 \pm \sqrt{64 + 192}}{12}$

$= \dfrac{8}{12} \pm \dfrac{16}{12}$

$r = \dfrac{-2}{3}$ or $x = 2$

PAPER C03 : FUNDAMENTALS OF BUSINESS MATHEMATICS

PROBABILITY

PROBABILITY THEORY

34 D

There is only one such card in the pack so probability is 1 in 52.

35 C

$$\frac{4}{10} \times \frac{3}{10} \times \frac{3}{10} = \frac{36}{100} \text{ or } 0.036$$

36 B

There are 13 hearts in a pack of 52 so $\frac{13}{52}$ or $\frac{1}{4}$

37 D

Independence

$$\frac{1}{6} \times \frac{1}{2} = \frac{1}{12}$$

38 B

Total number of females 500

Total number of students 1,500 so $\frac{500}{1,500} = \frac{1}{3}$.

39 C

Total number of failures

Total number of students $\frac{700}{1,500}$ so 7 in 15.

40 D

Turn question round

Someone who is not male and failed is a female who passed Total number of females who passed

$$\frac{\text{Total number of females who passed}}{\text{Total number of students}}$$

$$= \frac{300}{1,500} = 1 \text{ in } 5$$

Therefore the opposite = 4 in 5 or 0.8.

ANSWERS TO OBJECTIVE TEST QUESTIONS : SECTION 4

41 B

$$\frac{1,000}{1,500} \times \frac{500}{1,000} = \frac{2}{3} \times \frac{1}{2} = \frac{2}{6} \text{ or } \frac{1}{3}$$

so 1 in 3.

42 D

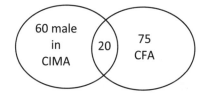

$$\left(\frac{60 + 75 - 20}{90 + 75}\right) = 0.70$$

43 A

$$\frac{4}{52} \times \frac{4}{51} \times \frac{4}{50} = \frac{8}{16575}$$

EXPECTED VALUE AND DECISION-MAKING

44 A

Product A expected value

= 0.4 × $600 + 0.6 × $100 = $240 + $60 = $300

Product B expected value

= 0.6 × $400 + 0.4 × –$50 = $240 – $20 = $220

Product A with higher expected value so A

45 D

Probability of having 0 defects is $\frac{(9)^6}{(10)^6} = 0.53$

46 D

0.3 × $10 + 0.3 × $50 + 0.4 × $80

= $3 + $15 + $32

= $50

47 C

$$\frac{0.8}{£400,000} - \frac{0.2}{£80,000} = \$320,000 - \$1,600$$

$$= \$304,000$$

PAPER C03 : FUNDAMENTALS OF BUSINESS MATHEMATICS

48   B AND C

If the newsagent purchased and sold 400 papers per day, his profit would be $60 (400 × 15p).

If the newsagent buys 400 but demand is 440 profit is still only $60 because he has only sold 400.

If the newsagent buys 440 the cost is $66 but if he only sells 400 X 30p his profit is reduced to $120 – $66 = $54.

So a pay off table would look like

Demand	Purchased per day			
	400	440	480	520
400	$60	$54	$48	$42
440	$60	$66	$60	$54
480	$60	$66	$72	$66
520	$60	$66	$72	$78

To calculate the expected value

Demand per day	Probability	Purchased per day			
		400	440	480	520
400	0.2	12	10.8	9.6	8.4
440	0.3	18	19.8	18.0	16.2
480	0.4	24	26.4	28.8	26.4
520	0.1	6	6.6	7.2	7.8
		60	63.6	63.6	58.8

Highest expected value 440 and 480 = $63.60.

49   B

Amount required = $50   winning number
                 + $50   profit
                 ─────
                 $100

No of tickets available = 40, so 100/40 gives $2.50 each

50   A

$$\frac{35}{37} \times 100 = 95\%$$

So on a $100 stake our rate of return is –5%.

ANSWERS TO OBJECTIVE TEST QUESTIONS : SECTION 4

51 C

The driver will pay a premium of $500 whether there is an accident or not so expected value =

premium of	$500
less 1% of $20,000	($200)
	$300

SUMMARISING AND ANALYSING DATA

PRESENTATION OF DATA

52 C

The statement which is correct is data + meaning = information.

53 A

Since we have multiplied one side by 1.5 we need to divide the other by 1.5 so 0.67.

54 B

There are 360 degrees in a circle

so $\frac{90}{360} \times \$550{,}000 = \$137{,}500$

55 C

Cumulative frequencies are plotted against the upper class boundaries.

56 C

Scale = 1 cm for 2 frequencies, then 28 should have a height of 14.

57 D

Simple, multiple, component and compound are all types of bar charts.

58 B

To be correctly presented, the histogram must show the relationship of the rectangles to the frequencies by reference to the area.

PAPER C03 : FUNDAMENTALS OF BUSINESS MATHEMATICS

AVERAGES

59 B

Arithmetic mean = $\dfrac{3+6+10+14+17+19+22}{7}$

60 C

Median is the value of the middle item. So there are three numbers below 14 and three numbers above.

61 B

Mean = 20 kg

Samples size = 10

so $15 + x + 22 + 14 + 21 + 15 + 20 + x + 18 + 27 = 200$

so $152 + 2x = 200$

$2x = 48$

$x = 24$

62 A

The mode is the value which appears with the highest frequency

63 B

Dept.	Mean wage	No of employees	Total
W	50	20	1,000
X	100	5	500
Y	70	10	700
Z	80	5	400
		40	2,600

Mean wage per employee – $\dfrac{£2,600}{40}$ = $65

64 A

If there are n items in the distribution the value of the median is $\dfrac{n+1}{2}$.

65 C

To make calculation easier subtract 500

So $500 + \dfrac{4+6+1+5+7+6+4+8+3+5+2+4}{12}$

$= 500 + \dfrac{55}{12} = 504.6$

ANSWERS TO OBJECTIVE TEST QUESTIONS : SECTION 4

66 B

Arranging in numerical order we have

501, 502, 503, 504, 504, 504, 505, 505, 506, 506, 507, 508

Median = $\dfrac{504 + 505}{2}$ = 504.5

67 A

It is 504 since it appears three times

68 D

The median is not suitable for mathematical statistics.

VARIATION

69 C

The coefficient of variation measures the relative dispersion of the given data, so C

70 A

x	x^2
3	9
5	25
8	64
11	121
13	169
$\Sigma 40$	$\Sigma x^2 = 388$

$\sigma = \sqrt{\dfrac{388}{5} - \left(\dfrac{40}{5}\right)^2}$

$= \sqrt{77.6 - 64}$

$= \sqrt{13.6}$

$= 3.69$

71 B

Coefficient of variation $= \dfrac{\text{Standard deviation} \times 100}{\text{Arithmetic mean}}$

$= \dfrac{1.1 \times 100}{3.5} = \dfrac{110}{3.5} = 31.43$

PAPER C03 : FUNDAMENTALS OF BUSINESS MATHEMATICS

72 D

Product A $\dfrac{10}{250} \times 100 = 4$

Product B $\dfrac{15}{250} \times 100 = 6$

Product C $\dfrac{20}{250} \times 100 = 8$

Product D $\dfrac{25}{250} \times 100 = 10$

so highest is Product D.

THE NORMAL DISTRIBUTION

73 D

$Z = \dfrac{380 - 360}{15} = 1.33$

From normal distribution table

Z = 0.4082

So probability > Z = 0.5 – 0.4082

= 0.0918

= 9%

74 B

$Z = \dfrac{330 - 360}{15} = -2$

From normal distribution table

Z = 0.4772

So probability Z < $330 = 0.5 – 0.4772

= 0.0228

= 2%

75 D

$Z = \dfrac{420 - 360}{15} = 4$

Highest value in the normal distribution table is 3.5, so it is impossible for worker to earn more than $420 from the data so no chance 0%.

ANSWERS TO OBJECTIVE TEST QUESTIONS : SECTION 4

76 D

Area between 330 and 360 = 0.4772 from Question 74.

$\dfrac{390 - 360}{15} = 2$ is also 0.4772

so 0.4722 + 0.4722 = 0.9544 so approximately 95%.

77 D

Required area is between 370 and 400

$\dfrac{400 - 360}{15} = 2.666 = 0.4962$

$\dfrac{370 - 360}{15} = 0.67 = 0.2486$

so 0.4962 − 0.2486 = 0.2476 or approximately 25%.

78 B

For an area of 0.49 Z = 2.33

$\dfrac{x - 360}{15} = \pm\, 2.33$

$360 + (\$15 \times 2.33) = \$394.95$

$360 - (\$15 \times 2.33) = \$325.05$

Middle 98% lies between $325.05 and $394.95.

79 D

From the normal distribution table, 30% of a distribution lies between the mean and 0.84 standard deviation above the mean

so $x = 150 + (0.84 \times 20)$

$= 166.8.$

80 C

If 6.68% of the population is above 180, then 0.5 − 0.0668 = 0.4332

so Z = 1.5

so $Z = \dfrac{x^1 - u}{\sigma} = 1.5$

$1.5 = \dfrac{(180 - 150)}{\sigma}$

$\sigma = \dfrac{30}{1.5}$

$= 20$

81

Odd–one–out is D since, in a normal distribution, the mean is equal to the mode which is equal to the median.

INDEX NUMBERS

82 A

Quarter	'Real' sales
1	$\frac{109}{100} \times 100 = 109.0$
2	$\frac{120}{110} \times 100 = 109.1$
3	$\frac{132}{121} \times 100 = 109.1$
4	$\frac{145}{133} \times 100 = 109.0$

The 'real' series is approximately constant and keeping up with inflation.

83 C

Current cost = $5 × 430 ÷ 150

84 A

($2,000 × 120 ÷ 160) = $1,500 = A

85 B

$$\text{All items index} = \frac{(50 \times 140)+(30 \times 130)+(20 \times 120)}{100} = 133$$

86 A

All items = food + non-food

$127 \times 10 = (? \times 3) + (130 \times 7)$

$1270 = 3? + 910$

$3? = 1270 - 910$

$3? = 360$

$? = 120$

87 A

$x \times \frac{112}{100} = 140$, so $x = \frac{140}{1.12} = 125$

88 C

In the base year, the price = (100/87) × £490 = £563.2183 ≈ £563.22

ANSWERS TO OBJECTIVE TEST QUESTIONS : SECTION 4

INTERRELATIONSHIP BETWEEN VARIABLES

CORRELATION AND REGRESSION

89 B

Equation of line is $y = a + bx$

$$b = \frac{(12 \times 14{,}200) - (560 \times 85)}{12 \times 62{,}500 - 560 \times 560} = \frac{122{,}800}{436{,}400}$$

$b = 0.281$

$$a = \frac{85}{12} - 0.281 \times \frac{560}{12} = -6.03$$

Regression line is $y = -6.03 + 0.281x$

90 B

$491 = 234 + 20b$

91 C

Fixed costs are $1,000; variable costs are $2.50

92 D

Student	Economics	Maths	D	D^2
A	4	2	2	4
B	5	3	2	4
C	2	1	1	1
D	1	4	-3	9
E	3	5	-2	4
F	6	6	0	0
				22

$1 - 6(2^2) = 1 - 132$

$6(36 - 1) = 210$

$= 1 - 0.63$

$= 0.37$

93 A

The variable to be predicted depends on some other variable.

94 A

Perfect positive linear, that is, rise by a constant amount

PAPER C03 : FUNDAMENTALS OF BUSINESS MATHEMATICS

95 B

The coefficient of determination (R^2) explains the percentage variation in the dependent variable which is explained by the independent variable.

96 C

$Y = a + bx$

$491 = 234 + 20b$

$b = \dfrac{491 - 234}{20} = 12.85$

97 A

In the equation $Y = a + bx$, a is equal to the intercept

98 B

For a perfect positive correlation we want the value of R to be equal to 1.

FORECASTING

TIME SERIES

99 C

$y = 7.112 + 3.949x$

seasonal variation = 1.12 × trend

for month 19

$y = 7.112 + (3.949 \times 19)\,1.12$

$y = 92$

100 B

The influence of booms and slumps in an industry is a measure of cyclical variations

101 B

Multiplicative model forecast = T × S

Sales last quarter 240 (Q_2)

Seasonality for Q_2 = +50%   S = 150

Trend = $\dfrac{240}{150} \times 100 = 160$ for Q_3

Seasonality = –50%   S = 50

Forecast = $160 \times \dfrac{50}{100} = 80$

ANSWERS TO OBJECTIVE TEST QUESTIONS : SECTION 4

102 C

Seasonally – adjusted data

$$= \frac{\text{Actual results}}{\text{Seasonal factor}}$$

$$= \frac{£25,000}{0.78} = £32,051$$

FINANCIAL MATHEMATICS

103 B

$(1 + r)^{12} = 1.253^{12}$

There are 12 months in a year.

so $1 + r = \sqrt[12]{1.253} = 1.019$

104 D

$1,000 (1 + cumulative factor for year 4 at 8%)

= $1,000 (1 + 3.312)

= $4,312

105 C

x = $5,000

$r = 8\% = \frac{8}{10} = 0.08$

$D = x(1 - r)^n$

= $5,000 × (1 – 0.08)^5

= $5,000 × 0.6591

= $3,295.

106 D

$1,200/1.12 = $1,071

$1,400/(1.12)^2 = $1,116

$1,600/(1.12)^3 = $1,139

$1,800/(1.12)^4 = $1,144

107 C

NPV = $1,000 (1 + 6.247)

= $1,000 × 7.247

= $7,247.

108 D

$A = \$1,200/1.08 = \$1,111.11$

$B = \$1,400/(1.08)^2 = \$1,200.27$

$C = \$1,600/(1.08)^3 = \$1,270.13$

$D = \$1,800/(1.08)^4 = \$1,323.05$

109 C

Check cumulative present value table

6% year 14	9.295	
6% year 4	3.465	subtract
	5.830	

$\$5,000 \times 5.830 = \$29,150.$

110 B

Let x = annual repayment

Present value of 8 repayments of x at 9% = $50,000

From tables $5.535 \times x = \$50,000$

$$x = \frac{£50,000}{5.535} = \$9,033$$

111 A

A real life example of this is a pension. In other words you are living off the interest and the capital remains.

$$\$4,000 \times \frac{1}{0.05} = \$80,000$$

112 B

$$PV = \frac{1}{V}$$

$$\$15,000 \times \frac{1}{0.06} = \$250,000$$

SPREADSHEETS

113 C

Working

The values of *y* first fall and then rise again symmetrically over the range of values given for *x*. This will result in a curve with a minimum point.

ANSWERS TO OBJECTIVE TEST QUESTIONS : **SECTION 4**

114 C

Working

The data in row 7 must not be included, otherwise the total will be treated as another result and will be allocated its own piece of pie. The range should only include those columns containing the actual data to be used.

115 D

Working

The use of absolute values is to be kept to a minimum as they do not change in line with changes in the assumptions which makes 'what–if?' analysis harder to perform.

116 C

Working

The formula =NOW() is typed into the required cell and the time and date as set on the computer will be inserted into the spreadsheet.

117 A

Working

= FORECAST is the function used to plot a regression line. The fixed cell references are necessary to ensure that each observation is compared with the whole range.

118 B

Working

Pareto analysis is based on the 80:20 rule, which can be expanded into a business setting, as the knowledge that a small number of items may take up a disproportionate amount of time. The above analysis of sales would identify the items that represent about 80% of revenue – the implication being that most business attention should focus on them.

119 A

Working

The initial investment must be expressed separately as it does not need to be discounted. It would otherwise be treated as the first year's cash flow. It must be deducted here because it has been expressed as a positive figure in the data table.

120 B

Working

Average is the Excel term used to calculate the ROI. Neither NPV nor IRR would require the figures to be divided by cell contents as in the formula here. The answer is rounded to two decimal places so the second blank must be 2.

Section 5

MOCK ASSESSMENT 1

1   Use the following data about the production of faulty or acceptable items in three departments to answer the probability questions. All items referred to in the questions are randomly selected from this sample of 250. Give all answers correct to four d.p.

	Department			
	P	Q	R	Total
Faulty	7	10	15	32
Acceptable	46	78	94	218
Total	53	88	109	250

   A   What is the probability that an item is faulty?

   Answer ....

   B   What is the probability that an item from department P is faulty?

   Answer ....

   C   What is the probability that an item found to be faulty comes from department P?

   Answer ....   (6 marks)

2   In an additive model, the seasonal variations given by averaging $Y - T$ values are 25, 18, −5 and −30. They have to be adjusted so that their total is 0. What is the value after adjustment of the average currently valued at −30?

   Answer ....   (2 marks)

3   Which of the following examples would constitute a multiple bar chart?

   A   Three adjacent bars then a gap then another three bars

   B   Six separate bars

   C   Two bars with a gap between them, each divided into three sections

   D   Any bar chart which displays more than one variable

   Answer ....   (2 marks)

4   If $\Sigma x = 500$, $\Sigma y = 200$, $\Sigma x^2 = 35{,}000$, $\Sigma y^2 = 9{,}000$, $\Sigma xy = 12{,}000$ and $n = 10$, calculate the product moment correlation coefficient to three d.p.

   Answer ....   (2 marks)

PAPER C03 : FUNDAMENTALS OF BUSINESS MATHEMATICS

5 Which of the following statements about standard deviation is incorrect?

   A   It measures variability
   B   It uses all the data
   C   It is not distorted by skewed data
   D   Its formula lends itself to mathematical manipulation

   Answer .... (2 marks)

6 An investment rises in value from $12,000 to $250,000 over 15 years. Calculate the percentage increase per year, to one d.p.

   Answer .... (2 marks)

7 Events P and Q are said to be independent. What does this mean?

   A   If P occurs, Q cannot occur
   B   If P occurs the probability of Q occurring is unchanged
   C   If P occurs the probability of Q occurring is 0
   D   If P occurs the probability of Q occurring is 1

   Answer .... (2 marks)

8 The following table shows the ranking of 5 countries in birth rate and growth rate. What is the coefficient of rank correlation?

Country	Birth Rate y	Growth Rate x
Brazil	30	5.1
Mexico	36	3.8
Taiwan	21	6.2
India	36	1.4
Sri Lanka	27	2.5

   A   1
   B   −0.66
   C   −0.33
   D   −1

   (4 marks)

9 Sales figures are given as 547,000 but after seasonal adjustment using a multiplicative model they are only 495,000. Calculate the seasonal component for the particular season, to 3 d.p.

   Answer .... (2 marks)

10 Solve the simultaneous equations:

$x + 3y = 14 \quad 2x - 3y = -8$

A $x = 6$ $y = 3$

B $x = 3$ $y = 6$

C $x = 2$ $y = 4$

D $x = 4$ $y = 2$

(2 marks)

11 If a sum of $15,000 is invested at 4.6 per cent per annum, find its value after 5 years, to the nearest –$.

Answer ………………… (2 marks)

12 A   Express the following average weekly wages as index numbers with base 1998, to 1 d.p.

Year	97	98	99	2000	2001	2002
RPI	166	172	178	184	190	197
Wages	414	426	440	450	468	480
Index	…	…	…	…	…	…

B   If the index for 2003 were to be 116 and the RPI 204, express the index for 2003 at constant 1998 prices.

C   If the average wages index for 2003 at constant 1998 prices were to be 96, which of the following comments would be correct?

   A   Average wages in 2003 could buy 4 per cent less than in 1998

   B   Average wages in 2003 could buy 4 per cent more than in 1998

   C   Average wages in 2003 were 4 per cent more than in 1998

   D   Average prices in 2003 were 4 per cent less than in 1998

   Answer ………………… (6 marks)

13 The expression $(x^3)^2 / x^4$ equals

A $1/x$

B 1

C x

D x^2

Answer ………………… (2 marks)

PAPER C03 : FUNDAMENTALS OF BUSINESS MATHEMATICS

14 Which of the following equations does not have straight line graphs?

    A $y = 7x + 5$

    B $y = \dfrac{13x - 5}{2}$

    C $y = 3x^2 + x$

    D $y = -19$

(2 marks)

15 The pass rate for a particular exam is 48 per cent. In a randomly selected group of three students, find the probabilities (to 4 d.p.) that

    A   No one passes

         Answer ....

    B   All three pass

         Answer ....

(4 marks)

16 A company has to choose between borrowing $100,000 at 3 per cent a quarter in order to modernise now or saving at 2 per cent a quarter in order to modernise in 4 years time, at an estimated cost of $117,000. Throughout this question, use tables whenever possible.

    A   Find the cumulative discount factor appropriate to quarter end payments of $1 per quarter at 3 per cent per quarter over 5 years

         Answer ....

    B   Calculate the amount $X which must be paid per quarter if the company borrows $100,000 now repayable at the end of each quarter over 4 years. Give your answer correct to the nearest $

         Answer ....

    C   Calculate the amount $Y which must be saved at the end of each quarter if the company wishes to cover the cost of modernisation in 4 years time. Give your answer to the nearest $

         Answer ....

(6 marks)

MOCK ASSESSMENT 1 : SECTION 5

17 Eight samples of wine have been listed in order of taste (with the best taste being ranked number one) and their prices are also listed.

Sample taste	1	2	3	4	5	6	7	8
Price GO	6.99	4.95	5,99	5.99	4.49	3,99	2,99	2.99
Rank of price	..	..	..	..	..	..	..	..

A Rank the prices of the wines with the lowest price being ranked number one

B If the differences in corresponding ranks are denoted by 'd' and if $\Sigma d^2 = 150$, calculate Spearman's rank correlation coefficient to 3 d.p.

Answer ....

C If the rank correlation coefficient was -0.9, which of the following statements would be correct?

    (i)   There is a strong link between price and taste.

    (ii)   There is a strong linear relationship between price and taste.

    (iii) Taste rank increases as price gets higher.

    (iv) 97 per cent of the differences in price from one sample to the next can be explained by corresponding differences in taste.

Answer(s) ....   (6 marks)

18 Calculate the present value of an annuity of $2,800 per annum, payable at the end of each year for 10 years at a discount rate of 4 per cent. Use tables and give your answer to the nearest $.

Answer ....   (2 marks)

19 An asset originally worth $80,000 depreciates at 28 per cent per annum. Find its value to the nearest $ at the end of 3 years.

Answer ....   (2 marks)

20 If the following data are to be illustrated by means of a histogram and if the standard interval is taken to be 5 seconds, calculate the heights of the bars of the histogram (to the nearest whole number).

Time taken (seconds)	Frequency	Height of bar
0–5	47	
5–10	62	
10–20	104	
20–40	96	

(4 marks)

21 In an additive time series model, at a certain point of time, the actual value is 32,000 while the trend is 26,000 and the seasonal component is 6,200. If there is no cyclical variation, calculate the residual variation.

Answer ....   (2 marks)

PAPER C03 : FUNDAMENTALS OF BUSINESS MATHEMATICS

22 Solve the equation $2x^2 - 5x - 7 = 0$ giving your answers correct to 1 d.p.

Answer .... (2 marks)

23 A project may result in the following profits with the probabilities stated.

Profit	Probability
$40,000	0.2
$25,000	0.4
($12,000)	0.4

Calculate the expected profit to the nearest $.

Answer .... (2 marks)

24 If weights are normally distributed with mean 43 kg and standard deviation 6 kg, what is the probability of a weight being less than 50 kg?

Answer .... (2 marks)

25 A sum of $30,000 is invested at a nominal rate of 12 per cent per annum. Find its value after 3 years if interest is compounded every month. Give your answer to the nearest $.

Answer .... (2 marks)

26 The three types of product sold by a shop have price indices of 105, 103 and 102 compared with last year. Find the weighted average index for the products, using quantities as weights if the quantities sold are in the ratio 3:2:1.

Answer .... (to 1 d.p.) (2 marks)

27 If $\Sigma x = 400$, $\Sigma y = 300$, $\Sigma x^2 = 18,000$, $\Sigma y^2 = 10,000$, $\Sigma xy = 13,000$ and $n = 10$,

    A   Calculate the value of 'b' in the regression equation, to 1 d.p.

    B   If the value of b were 0.9, calculate the value of 'a' in the regression equation to 1 d.p.

Answers

A   ....

B   .... (4 marks)

28 In a time series analysis, the trend Y is given by the regression equation $Y = 462 + 0.34t$ where t denotes the quarters of years with 1st quarter of 2000 as $t = 1$.

    A   Predict the trend for the first quarter of 2004 to one d.p.

        Answer ....

    B   If the average seasonal variations are as follow

Quarter	Q1	Q2	Q3	Q4
Variation	20%	0	−20%	+40%

Use the multiplicative model to predict the actual value for a 3rd quarter in which the trend prediction is 500.

        Answer .... (4 marks)

MOCK ASSESSMENT 1 : SECTION 5

29 A sales representative calls on three separate, unrelated customers and the chance of making a sale at any one of them is 0.7. Find the probability that a sale is made on the third call only, to 3 d.p.

Answer .... (2 marks)

30 Rearrange the formula $V = P \times (1 + r)^n$ to make r the subject.

Answer .... (2 marks)

31 In November, unemployment in a region is 238,500. If the seasonal component using an additive time series model is – 82,000, find the seasonally adjusted level of unemployment to the nearest whole number.

Answer .... (2 marks)

32 A company is planning capital investment for which the following year end cash flows have been estimated.

Year end	Net cash flow
Now	(10,000)
1	5,000
2	5,000
3	3,000

A   Use tables to calculate the net present value (NPV) of the project using tables if the company has a cost of capital of 15 per cent.

Answer ....

B   If the NPV is $928 when the discount rate is 10 per cent and – $628 when it is 20 per cent, calculate the internal rate of return to two d.p.

Answer .... (4 marks)

33 If the regression equation (in $'000) linking sales (Y) to advertising expenditure (X) is given by Y = 4,000 + 12X, forecast the sales when $150,000 is spent on advertising, to the nearest $.

Answer .... (2 marks)

34 An item sells for $4.39 including value added tax at 17.5 per cent. If tax were reduced to 16 per cent, the new selling price to the nearest penny will be

A $4.33

B $4.01

C $4.32

D $5.09

Answer .... (2 marks)

PAPER C03 : FUNDAMENTALS OF BUSINESS MATHEMATICS

35 If $\Sigma f = 50$, $\Sigma fx = 120$ and $\Sigma fx^2 = 400$, calculate

    A   The mean (to 1 d.p.)

        Answer ....

    B   The standard deviation (to 1 d.p.)

        Answer ....   **(4 marks)**

36 The Economic Order Quantity (EOQ) for a particular stock item is given by the expression:

$$EOQ = \sqrt{\frac{2C_o D}{C_h}}$$

  (A) If $C_o = \$2$ per order, $D = 1{,}000$ items and $C_h = \$0.25$ per item, then EOQ (rounded to the nearest whole number) will be

      A   400

      B   320

      C   160

      D   126

      Answer ....

  (B) If, for a different stock item, EOQ = 200 items, $C_o = \$4$ per order and $D = 1{,}000$ items, then C_h (in \$ per item) will be

      A   0.05

      B   0.10

      C   0.15

      D   0.20

        Answer ....   **(4 marks)**

37 A graphical presentation of classified data in which the number of items in each class is represented by the area of the bar is called

    A   an ogive

    B   a histogram

    C   a bar chart

    D   a compound bar chart

    Answer ....   **(2 marks)**

38 The following table shows the index of prices (1995 = 100) for a certain commodity over the period 2000–2005

2000	2001	2002	2003	2004	2005
100	105	115	127	140	152

(A) The percentage increase in the price between 2002 and 2004 is nearest to

    A   25.0

    B   22.3

    C   21.7

    D   none of these

    Answer …………………   **(2 marks)**

(B) It has been decided to rebase the index so that 2003 = 100. The index for 2005 will now be nearest to

    A   193.1

    B   139.4

    C   125.0

    D   119.7

    Answer …………………   **(2 marks)**

39 The cost of an office desk is $263 plus value added tax of 17.5 per cent. Using the numbers given what Excel formula is required to calculate the total price to 2 d.p.?

Answer …………………   **(2 marks)**

40

	A	B	C	D	E
1	IT Investment – Cash Out		250000		
2	Net IT Benefits	Year 1		66000	
3		Year 2		87000	
4		Year 3		98000	
5		Year 4		120000	
6		Year 5		110000	
7					
8	Fixed Cost of Capital or Interest Rate			24%	
9					
10	ROI				
11	NPV				

Given the scenario in the spreadsheet above, what Excel formulae are required in

    A   Cell D10 to calculate the ROI

        Answer …………………

    B   Cell D11 to calculate the NPV

        Answer …………………   **(4 marks)**

PAPER C03 : FUNDAMENTALS OF BUSINESS MATHEMATICS

41

	A	B	C	D	E
1	INTEREST RATES AND CASH DEPOSITS				
2					
3	Interest rate	Deposit		Forecast	
4	10.00%	11550			
5	10.25%	11900			
6	10.50%	12500			
7	10.50%	11990			
8	10.75%	12900			
9	11.00%	13000			
10	11.25%	14000			
11	11.25%	13020			
12	11.25%	14000			
13	11.25%	14100			
14	11.50%	13380			
15	11.50%	14200			
16	11.75%	13500			
17	11.75%	14050			
18	12.00%	14500			
19	12.00%	14100			
20	12.25%	14500			
21	12.25%	14600			

Given the scenario above, what Excel formula is required in cell d4 to calculate the forecast (using a least squared line approach)? Write your answer so that the formula can be copied into cells D5 through D21.

Answer .... **(2 marks)**

42

	A	B	C	D	E	F	G
1	Average weight of pallets						
2	73	62	66	75	70	71	
3	83	E3	74	79	78	82	
4	65	72	66	79	82	77	
5	63	61	63	80	82	66	
6	82	82	65	75	71	80	
7	74	84	72	7B	67	84	
8							
9	Weight in kg						
10	60						
11	65						
12	70						
13	75						
14	80						
15	85						
16							

Given the scenario above, what Excel formula is required in the range b10:b15 to calculate the frequency distribution of the pallet weights?

Answer ………………… **(2 marks)**

43

	A	B	C	D	E
1	Average daily temperature in degrees centigrade			
2	29	25	22	29	
3	24	26	25	28	
4	28	27	20	22	
5	21	20	24	24	
6	21	22	27	26	
7	23	26	21	24	
8	25	25	24	25	
9					
10	Median				
11	Mode				
12	Mean				
13					

Given the scenario above, what Excel formulae are required to calculate?

A   The median (to 1 d.p.)

       Answer …………………

B   The mode (to 0 d.p.)

       Answer …………………

C   The mean (to 2 d.p.)

       Answer ………………… **(3 marks)**

44 Solve for y in the following inequalities.

(a) $-5x + 10y + 120 \geq 25x + 5y + 320$

Answer ....

(b) $240 + 8x \leq 12x - 10y + 140$

Answer .... **(2 marks)**

45 (a) Describe the shaded area in the following Venn diagram.

A   Even numbers which begin with 3

B   Numbers that are even but do not have a 3 in them

C   The numbers 6, 12, 24, 30, 36

D   None of the above

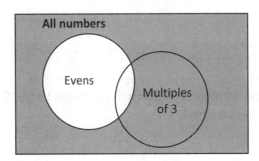

Answer ....

(b) If 50 people were asked whether they liked apples or oranges or both, 38 liked apples and 32 liked oranges. Use a Venn diagram to help you calculate how many people liked both?

A   10

B   15

C   20

D   25 **(8 marks)**

Section 6

MOCK ASSESSMENT 2

1. **$1,000 is to be shared between Christopher, Martin and Cameron in the ratio 24:22:14. How much does Martin receive?**

    A $265.54

    B $325.68

    C $366.67

    D $421.25

2. **If a good is priced at $745, including a sales tax of 17.5%, what is the price of the product excluding tax?**

    A $620.38

    B $634.04

    C $661.17

    D $685.42

3. **A table has five rows showing exam results and three columns showing schools in a town. Which of the following charts could be used to show the data?**

    (i)   A single pie chart

    (ii) A multiple bar chart

    (iii) A simple bar chart

    (iv) A component bar chart

    A   (i) and (ii)

    B   (ii) and (iii)

    C   (i) and (iv)

    D   (ii) and (iv)

PAPER C03 : FUNDAMENTALS OF BUSINESS MATHEMATICS

Questions 4 and 5 are based on the following data

The exam results for seven students were: 50, 55, 43, 52, 43, 62, 43.

4　The value of the mode is:

    A　43

    B　50

    C　52

    D　55

5　The median of the exam marks is:

    A　43

    B　50

    C　52

    D　55

6　What is the simplest way to express $2a^2 \times 3a^3$?

    A　$5a^5$

    B　$5a^6$

    C　$6a^5$

    D　$6a^6$

7　If a = 2 and b = 4, x = 6 and y = 10, then $\frac{a}{x} + \frac{b}{y}$ is equal to:

    A　$\frac{8}{10}$

    B　$\frac{13}{60}$

    C　$\frac{11}{15}$

    D　$\frac{15}{16}$

Questions 8 and 9 are based on the following data

A bookshop sells a book for $25, which they buy in for $15.

8　The gross profit is:

    A　25%

    B　40%

    C　50%

    D　60%

9 The profit mark–up is:

   A 50%
   B 60%
   C 66.66%
   D None of the above

10 A student obtained 68% in a piece of coursework, 50% in his first exam and 48% in the final exam. The weightings were 20% coursework, 30% for exam 1 and 50% in the final exam. His result for the course was:

   A 48%
   B 50%
   C 52.6%
   D 55.4%

11 Solve the equation $2x^2 - 3x - 7 = 0$ using the formula $\dfrac{-b \pm \sqrt{b^2 - 4ac}}{2a}$

   A 2.766 or – 1.266
   B –2.766 or 1.266
   C 1.266 or – 1.266
   D –2.766 or – 2.766

12 A product has been reduced in price from $105.28 to $94.11. To two decimal places, the percentage reduction in price was:

   A 11%
   B 10.6%
   C 10.61%
   D 10.62%

13 If fixed cost is $5,000 and variable cost is equal to $100, then the formula for total cost may be written as:

   A 100 + 5,000x
   B 100 + 5,100x
   C $5,000 + 5,100x
   D $5,000 + 100x

PAPER C03 : FUNDAMENTALS OF BUSINESS MATHEMATICS

14 If $6x + 8y = 50$ and $20x + 4y = 76$, then the values of x and y are:

- A $x = 3: y = 4$
- B $x = 4: y = 5$
- C $x = 6: y = 4$
- D $x = 5: y = 6$

Questions 15 and 16 are based on the following information

A pack of cards consists of 52 playing cards divided into four suits of 13; hearts, diamonds, clubs and spades.

15 What is the probability that a card selected at random is the queen of hearts?

- A 1 in 52
- B 1 in 26
- C 1 in 13
- D 1 in 4

16 What is the probability of choosing three cards from the same suit in succession, assuming that once a card is picked it is not returned to the pack?

- A 1%
- B 3%
- C 5%
- D 7%

17 A basket of fruit contains 3 oranges, 2 apples and 5 bananas. If a piece of fruit is chosen random, what is the probability of getting an apple or a banana?

- A $\dfrac{1}{2}$
- B $\dfrac{2}{5}$
- C $\dfrac{15}{100}$
- D $\dfrac{7}{10}$

18 A school is having a prize draw offering a $500 holiday to the winner. The tickets are on sale for 50p. If the $500 holiday was given to the school by a local travel company for $300, how many tickets would they need to sell to make a profit of $250. There are no other expenses.

   A   950
   B   1,000
   C   1,050
   D   1,100

19 A restaurant is opening a new store in 2 locations with 0.7 chance of making a $300,000 profit p.a. and a 0.3 chance of incurring a $50,000 loss. The expected value of these sites is:

   A $195,000
   B $205,000
   C $225,000
   D $245,000

20 Which of the following is not a bar chart?

   A   Simple
   B   Component
   C   Multiple
   D   Pie

21 Which one of the following has been incorrectly algebraically simplified?

   A $\dfrac{x^3}{-x^2} = -x$
   B $(3a^2b) \times (-a^3b^2c) = -3a^5b^3c$
   C $(1-x)(x+3) = -x^2 + 2x + 3$
   D $3x(x+2) - 7x^2 = -4x^2 + 6x$

22 Peter put $1000 in the bank. However, the interest rate he gets is floating year to year with 3%, 3.5% and 3.2% respectively. He reinvests the interest he receives at the end of each year. How much is Peter going to get by the end of year three? (Round to 2 d.p)

   A   = $1097.00
   B   = $1100.16
   C   = $1110.16
   D   = $1132.00

PAPER C03 : FUNDAMENTALS OF BUSINESS MATHEMATICS

23 In a pie chart, if wages are represented by 60° and the total cost is $720,000, the amount paid out in wages is:

- A $60,000
- B $120,000
- C $150,000
- D $180,000

24 Which of the following is not an advantage of using the mean?

- A It is easy to calculate
- B All the data in the distribution is used
- C It can be used in more advanced mathematical statistics
- D It is not affected by extreme values

25 If the standard deviation is 1.2 and the arithmetic mean is 3.6, then the coefficient of variation is:

- A 3
- B 33.33
- C 66.66
- D 99.99

26 The standard deviation of 3, 5, 7, 8, 9, 11 is:

- A 2.2
- B 2.4
- C 2.6
- D 3.0

27 A normal distribution has a mean of 150 and a standard deviation of 20. 70% of this distribution is below:

- A 155.4
- B 158.3
- C 160.6
- D 172.5

28 In a normal distribution with a mean of 100, 7% of the population is above 120. The standard deviation of the distribution is:

- A 10
- B 13.51
- C 16.67
- D 20

Questions 29–31 are based on the following information

The average income of a country is known to be $15,000 with standard deviation $2,000.

29 What is the probability of an average income over $19,000?

- A 2%
- B 3%
- C 4%
- D 5%

30 What is the probability of an average income less than $12,000?

- A 14%
- B 6.7%
- C 17%
- D 19%

31 What is the probability that the average income is between $12,000 and $19,000?

- A 16%
- B 9%
- C 18%
- D 19%

32 What is the NPV of buying an asset that will generate income of $1,200 at the end of each year for eight years? The price of the asset is $6,200 and the annual interest rate is 10%.

- A −$202
- B $202
- C $3,400
- D −$1,721.53

33 In a forecasting model based on $Y - a$ and bx, the intercept is $250. If the value of $Y = \$495$ and $x = 25$, then b is equal to:

- A 9.80
- B 15
- C 17.50
- D 25.75

PAPER C03 : FUNDAMENTALS OF BUSINESS MATHEMATICS

34 The coefficient of determination r^2 explains the:

    A   Percentage variation in the dependent variable, which is explained by the independent variable

    B   The relationship between the two variables

    C   The gradient, the intercept and the coefficient

    D   None of the above

35 A new vehicle costs $20,000. It is depreciated by 25% per annum on a reducing balance. At the end of year 3, the book value will be:

    A $11,250.75

    B $9,750.25

    C $8,750.50

    D $8,437.50

36 How much needs to be invested now at 5% to yield an annual income of $8,000 in perpetuity?

    A $12,000

    B $140,000

    C $160,000

    D $200,000

37 A landlord receives a rent of $1,000 to be received over ten successive years. The first payment is due now. If interest rates are 8%, then the present value of this income is equal to:

    A $6,951

    B $7,345

    C $7,247

    D $8,138

38 What is the annual repayment on a bank loan of $100,000 over 10 years at 7%?

    A $13,141

    B $14,237

    C $15,123

    D $16,981

Questions 39 and 40 are based on the following data

In a time series, the multiplicative model is used to forecast sales and the following seasonal variations apply:

Quarter	1	2	3	4
Seasonal variation	1.2	1.8	0.6	?

The actual sales for the first two quarters of 2008 were:

Quarter 1 $110,000

Quarter 2 $125,000

39 The seasonal variation to the fourth quarter is:

    A   0.2

    B   0.4

    C   0.6

    D   0.8

40 The trend line for sales:

    A   Decreased between quarter 1 and quarter 2

    B   Increased between quarter 1 and quarter 2

    C   Remained constant between quarter 1 and quarter 2

    D   Cannot be determined from the information given

41

	A	B	C	D	E
1					
2	Amount invested	258000			
3	Cash flow year 1	73000			
4	Cash flow year 2	32000			
5	Cash flow year 3	27000			
6	Cash flow year 4	12000			
7					
8	Fixed cost of capital	15%			

Given the above data, which of the following Excel functions and formula will calculate the ROI of the investment?

    A   =ROI(B3:B6)/B2

    B   =AVERAGE(B3:B6)–B2

    C   =AVERAGE(B3:B6)/B2

    D   =ROI(B3:B6)/B2*B8

(2 marks)

PAPER C03 : FUNDAMENTALS OF BUSINESS MATHEMATICS

42 To find the mean of a number of values in a range labelled with the name OBSERVATIONS in an Excel spreadsheet, the following command should be entered into the required cell:

A = MEDIAN(OBSERVATIONS)

B = MEAN(OBSERVATIONS)

C = MODE(OBSERVATIONS)

D = AVERAGE(OBSERVATIONS) (2 marks)

43 How would the calculation of the 6th root of 98 be entered into a spreadsheet?

A =98^1/6

B =98^(1/6)

C =1/6^98

D =(1/6)^98

44 In the Excel spreadsheet below, cell B6 is called the:

A work cell

B current cell

C active cell

D key cell

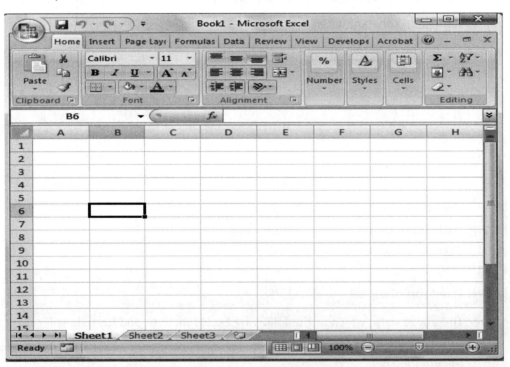

45 **The following function has been typed into a cell within an Excel spreadsheet:**

=IF(D6<>D7,"error","OK")

This is an example of:

A   an error message

B   a protected cell

C   what-if analysis

D   a control check

Section 7

ANSWERS TO MOCK ASSESSMENT 1

1 A 32 out of 250 items are faulty

Answer = 32/250 = 0.128

B 7 of the 53 items from P are faulty

Answer = 7/53 = 0.1321 (4 d.p.).

C 7 out of the 32 faulty items come from P

Answer = 7/32 = 0.2188 (4 d.p.).

2 Total = 25 + 18 − 5 − 30 = 8

If we subtract 2 from each of the four averages they will add up to zero.

Answer: − 30 − 2 = − 32

3 **A**

(B) describes a simple bar chart and (C) describes a compound or component bar chart. (D) is incorrect because a compound bar also shows several variables.

4 **0.283**

$r = [n\Sigma xy - \Sigma x \Sigma y] / \sqrt{\{[n\Sigma x^2 - (\Sigma x)^2] \times [n\Sigma y^2 - (\Sigma y)^2]\}}$

$= [10 \times 12{,}000 - 500 \times 200] / \sqrt{\{[10 \times 35{,}000 - 500^2][10 \times 9{,}000 - 200^2]\}}$

$= 20{,}000 / \sqrt{\{100{,}000 \times 50{,}000\}} = 0.283$ (3 d.p.)

5 **C**

Standard deviation uses all the data in a mathematically exact formula as a means of measuring variability. However, its one big disadvantage is that it greatly exaggerates the dispersion of skewed data so (C) is incorrect.

6 22.4

15 year ratio = 250/12 = 20.83333

1 year ratio = $20.83333^{(1/15)}$ = 1.2244

Annual % increase = 22.4%

7 B

Events are independent if the occurrence of one does not alter the probability of the other, so (B) is correct. (A) and (C) are both definitions of mutually exclusive events.

8 C

Country	Birth rate y	Growth rate x	Rank y	Rank x	D	D^2
Brazil	30	5.1	2.5	2	0.5	0.25
Mexico	36	3.8	1	3	−2	4
Taiwan	21	6.2	5	1	4	16
India	30	1.4	2.5	5	−2.5	6.25
Sri Lanka	27	2.3	4	4	0	0

$$r = \frac{6 \times \Sigma D^2}{n \times (n^2 - 1)} \qquad \Sigma D^2 = 26.5$$

$$r = 1 - \frac{6 \times 26.5}{5 \times (5^2 - 1)} = 0.325 = 0.33$$

9 1.105

Seasonally adjusted value = actual value/seasonal component. So seasonal component = actual value divided by seasonally adjusted value = 547/495 = 1.105

10 C

$x + 3y = 14$ (1)

$2x - 3y = -8$ (2)

Eq. (1) + (2)

$3x = 6$

So that $x = 2$

To find y we substitute $x = 2$ into either equation.

$2 + 3y = 14, \Rightarrow 3y = 14 - 2 = 12$

$\Rightarrow y = \dfrac{12}{13} = 4$

11 $18,782

Value = $15{,}000 \times 1.046^5$ = $18,782

ANSWERS TO MOCK ASSESSMENT 1 : SECTION 7

12 **97.8**

(A) Wages are indexed with base 98 by dividing each year's wages figure by the '98 figure (i.e. by 426) and multiplying by 100.

Answers

97	98	99	00	01	02
91.2	100	103.3	105.6	109.9	112.7

(B) Value at '98 prices = 116 × 98 RPI/'03 RPI = 116 × 172/204 = 97.8

(C) An index of 96 means a drop of 4 per cent and, in this case, the drop is in the quantity of goods and services which the average wage buys. So the answer is (A). **Answer: (A)**

13 **D**

$(x^3)^2/x^4 = x^6/x^4 = x^{(6-4)} = x^2$

14 **C**

A – the form of a straight line is $y = mx + c$ where m and c are constants. Here $y = 7x + 5$ is an equation of the form where m = 7 and c = 5. This equation has a straight line.

B – the equation – $y = \dfrac{13x - 5}{2}$ can be written as $y = \dfrac{13x}{2} - \dfrac{5}{2}$, which is in the form $y = mx + c$ with $m = \dfrac{13}{2}$ and $c = \dfrac{-5}{2}$

C – $y = 3x^2 + x$ contains the term x^2. Such a term is not allowed in the equation of a straight line.

D – $y = -19$ is in the form of the equation of a straight line for which m = 0 and c = 19.

15 Probability of failing is 1 – 0.48 = 0.52

A Probability of all three failing = 0.52^3 = 0.1406

Answer: 0.1406

B Probability of all three passing = 0.48^3 = 0.1106

Answer: 0.1106

16 (A) There are 20 quarterly payments in 5 years, so the discount factor required is that corresponding to 3 per cent and 20 periods.

Answer: 14.878

(B) The method is to equate the present value of the repayments with the 100,000 borrowed. The cumulative discount factor at 3 per cent for 16 periods is 12.561 so

100,000 = 12.561X

X = 100,000/12.561 = $7,961 (to the nearest $)

Answer: 7,961

PAPER C03 : FUNDAMENTALS OF BUSINESS MATHEMATICS

(C) The present value of the saving scheme must be equated to that of $117,000 discounted at 2 per cent for 16 periods. The cumulative discount factor is 13.578 whilst the single discount factor is 0.728. Hence 13.578 Y = 117,000 X 0.728 and Y = $6,273 (to nearest $).

Answer: 6,273

17   A   **Answer:** 8 5 6.5 6.5 4 3 1.5 1.5

       B   R = 1 − 6Σd^2/n(n^2 − 1) = 1 − 6 × 150/8 × 63 = − 0.786 (to 3 d.p.)

          Answer: − 0.786

       C   The value 0.9 means that there is a strong link between taste and price but it need not be linear. Because of the strange way in which taste is ranked, with the lowest rank being the best taste, rank of taste actually declines as price increases. **Answer:** (iv)

18   The cumulative discount factor for 10 years at 4 per cent is 8.111, so the present value is 2,800 × 8.111 = $22,711 (to the nearest $)

      Answer: 22,711

19   If something declines at 28% per year, its value at the end of each year is only 72 per cent of its value at the start, so year–end value is start value times 0.72. Value after 3 years = 80,000 × 0.72^3 = $29,860 (to the nearest $)

      Answer: 29,860

20   If the width of an interval is n times the standard width, then the height of its bar is frequency/n.

      Heights are 47, 62, 104/2 = 52 and 96/4 = 24.

      Answers: 47, 62, 52, 24

21   **−200**

      The formula for an additive time series is A = T + S + R and hence residual = A − T− S = 32,000 − 26,000 − 6,200 = − 200

22   Using the formula for the roots of a quadratic, a = 2, b = −5 and c = −7 to give

      x = (5 ± 9)/ 4

      Alternately, factorisation gives (2x − 7)(x + 1) = 0 and hence x = −1 or 3.5

      Answers: −1, 3.5

23   Expected profit ($000) = 40 × 0.2 + 25 X 0.4 − 12 × 0.4 = 13.2

      Answer: 13,200

ANSWERS TO MOCK ASSESSMENT 1 : SECTION 7

24 $P(W < 50) = P(z < [50 - 43]/6) = P(z < 1.17)$

$\qquad$ = 0.5 + Normal table entry for 1.17 = 0.5 + 0.3790

$\qquad$ = 0.8790

Answer: 0.8790

25 A nominal 12 per cent per annum means 1 per cent per month and in 3 years there are 36 months. Value = $30{,}000 \times 1.01^{36}$ = \$42,923 (to the nearest \$).

Answer: 42,923

26 **103.8**

Weighted average index = $(3 \times 105 + 2 \times 103 + 1 \times 102)/(3+2+1)$ = 103.8

27 (A) $\quad 'b' = [n\Sigma xy - \Sigma x \Sigma y]/[n\Sigma x^2 - (\Sigma x)^2]$

$\qquad\quad$ = $[10 \times 13{,}000 - 400 \times 300]/[10 \times 18{,}000 - 400^2]$ = 10,000/20,000 = 0.5

Answer: 0.5

(B) $\quad 'a' = \Sigma y/n - b \times \Sigma x/n = [300 - 0.9 \times 400]/10 = -6$

Answer: −6

28 (A) For the 1st quarter of 2004, $t = 17$ and trend $Y = 462 + 0.34 \times 17 = 467.8$ (to 1 d.p.)

Answer: 467.8

(B) Prediction = trend prediction reduced by 20% = 500×0.8

Answer: 400

29 P(not making a sale) = $1 - P$(making a sale) = $1 - 0.7 = 0.3$

P(sale at 3rd call only) = P(*not* at 1st) × P(not at 2nd) × P(sale at 3rd) = $0.3 \times 0.3 \times 0.7 = 0.063$

Answer: 0.063

30 $(1 + r)^n = V/P$ so $1 + r = (V/P)^{(1/n)}$ and $r = (V/P)^{(1/n)} - 1$

Answer: $(V/P)^{(1/n)} - 1$

31 The additive model is $A = T + S$ and seasonal adjustment provides an estimate of $T = A - S =$ 238,500 − (− 82,000) = 238,500 + 82,000

Answer: 320,500

PAPER C03 : FUNDAMENTALS OF BUSINESS MATHEMATICS

32 (A)

Year	Cash flow	Discount factor	Present value
0	(10,000)	1	(10,000)
1	5,000	0.87	4,350
2	5,000	0.756	3,780
3	3,000	0.658	1,974
			NPV = 104

Answer: 104

(B) The IRR is the rate at which NPV is zero. NPV drops by $928 + $628 = $1,556 as the percentage rises from 10 per cent to 20 per cent that is by 10 per cent points. The drop per point is therefore 1,556/10 = $155.6. Since it starts at $928, the NPV will reach zero after an increase in the rate of 928/155.6 = 5.96% points. This occurs when the rate = 10 + 5.96 = 15.96% (to 2 d.p.)

Answer: 15.96

33 **$5,800,000**

When $150,000 is spent on advertising, $X = 150$ and $Y = 4,000 + 12 \times 150 = 5,800$. Forecast sales = 5,800 ($000).

34 **A**

Price with VAT at 17.5% = 1.175 × Price without VAT

So price without VAT = 4.39/1.175

Price with VAT at 16% = 1.16 × Price without VAT = 1.16 × 4.39/1.175 = $4.33

35 (A) Mean = $\Sigma fx/\Sigma f$ = 120/50 – 2.4

Answer: 2.4

(B) Standard deviation = $\sqrt{[\Sigma fx^2 / \Sigma f - (\Sigma fx/\Sigma f)^2]} = \sqrt{[400/50 - (120/50)^2]}$

$= \sqrt{2.24}$ = 1.5 (to 1 d.p.)

Answer: 1.5

ANSWERS TO MOCK ASSESSMENT 1 : SECTION 7

36 (A) $EOQ = \sqrt{\dfrac{2C_0 D}{C_h}}$

$C_0 = 2$, $D = 1,000$, $C_h = 0.25$

$\therefore EOQ = \sqrt{\dfrac{2 \times 2 \times 1,000}{0.25}} = \sqrt{\dfrac{4,000}{0.25}} = \sqrt{16,000}$

$\therefore$ EOQ = 126.49 = 126 to nearest whole number

Answer: D

(B) EOQ = 200, C0 = 4, D = 1000

$\therefore 200 = \sqrt{\dfrac{2 \times 4 \times 1,000}{C_h}} = \sqrt{\dfrac{8,000}{C_h}}$

$\therefore 200^2 = \dfrac{8,000}{C_h}$

$\therefore C_h = \dfrac{8,000}{40,000} = 0.20$

Answer: D

37 **B**

An ogive doesn't have bars. A bar chart looks similar to a histogram but in a bar chart the height of the bar represents the frequency. In a histogram this is only the case if the classes are of equal width. In general the area of the bar in a histogram represents class frequency.

38 (A) % increase between 2002 and 2004:

$\left(\dfrac{140 - 115}{115}\right) \times 100 = \dfrac{25}{115} \times 100 = 21.74$

Answer: C

(B) Rebased price

$\dfrac{152}{127} \times 100 = 119.69$

Answer: (D)

39 **A**

Answer: = ROUND (263 × 1.175,2)

= 309.03 (2 d.p)

40 A **Answer:** = AVERAGE(D2:D6)/C1

B **Answer:** = NPV(D8,D2:D6) − C1

41 **Answer:** = FORECAST(A4,$B$4:$B$31,$A$4:$A$31)

PAPER C03 : FUNDAMENTALS OF BUSINESS MATHEMATICS

42   **Answer:**   = FREQUENCY(A2:F7,A10:A14)

43   **Answer:**   = ROUND(MEDIAN(A2:D8),1)

   Answer: = ROUND(MODE(A2:D8),0)

   Answer: = ROUND(AVERAGE(A2:D8),2)

44   (A) $10y - 5y \geq 25x + 5x + 200$

   $5y \geq 30x + 200$

   $Y \geq 6x + 40$

   (B) $-10y \leq 12x - 8x + 140 - 240$

   $-10y \leq 4x - 100$

   $-y \leq 0.4x - 10$

   $Y \geq -0.4x + 10$

45   (a)   **Answer:** D

   (b)   **Answer:** C

Section 8

ANSWERS TO MOCK ASSESSMENT 2

1   **C**

24 + 22 + 14 = 60

$\frac{22}{60} \times \$1,000 = 366.67$

2   **B**

$\frac{£745}{1,175} = \$634.04$

3   **D**

A simple bar chart and a simple pie chart could not hold this amount of information. So D – (ii) and (iv).

4   **A**

The mode is the value which appears the most frequently, so 43 appears 3 times.

5   **B**

The median is the value of the middle item in a distribution. There are 3 marks above 50 and 3 marks below, so 50 is mode.

6   **C**

We need to multiply the numbers and add the powers, so $2a^2 \times 3a^3$ becomes $6a^5$.

7   **C**

$\frac{2}{6} + \frac{4}{10} = \frac{10}{30} + \frac{12}{30} = \frac{22}{30} = \frac{11}{15}$

8   **B**

Gross profit is % of sales

So $\frac{10}{25} = 40\%$

PAPER C03 : FUNDAMENTALS OF BUSINESS MATHEMATICS

9 C

The profit mark-up is the % mark-up on cost = 10/15 = 66.67%

10 C

0.2 × 68 + 0.3 × 50 + 0.5 × 48

$$\begin{array}{r} 13.6 \\ 15.0 \\ 24.0 \\ \hline 52.6 \\ \hline \end{array}$$

11 A

In this example $a = 2$, $b = -3$ and $c = -7$. Care should be taken with the negative signs. Substituting these into the formula, we find:

$$x = \frac{-b \pm \sqrt{b^2 - 4ac}}{2a}$$

$$= \frac{3 \pm \sqrt{9 - 4(2)(-7)}}{4}$$

$$= \frac{3 \pm \sqrt{65}}{4}$$

$$= \frac{3 \pm 8.062}{4}$$

= 2.766 or –1.266

12 C

100 × (105.28 – 94.11)/105.28 = 100 × 11.17/105.28 = 10.6098

Answer is 10.61, so C.

13 D

$5,000 + 100x

Total cost is fixed cost plus variable cost. Fixed cost remains at the same level regardless of output.

ANSWERS TO MOCK ASSESSMENT 2 : **SECTION 8**

14 A

6x + 8y = 50 ...(1)

20x + 4y = 76...(2)

Multiply equation (2) by 2 gives

40x + 8y = 152...(3)

Subtracting equation (1) from (3)

34x = 102

x = 3

Substituting back in (1) gives

18+8y =50

8y = 32

x = 3, y = 4

15 A

There are 4 queens, there are 13 hearts but only 1 queen of hearts, so 1 in 52. Answer A.

16 C

The first card picked could be from any suit but there will be only 12 left of that suit from 51 when we draw the second card, and 11 from 50 when we draw the third, so:

$$\frac{12}{51} \times \frac{11}{50} = \frac{132}{2,550}$$

Answer 0.05 or 5%

17

Answer D – Independent.

P (A o rB) = P (A) + P (B)

$$= \frac{2}{10} + \frac{5}{10}$$

$$= \frac{7}{10}$$

18 D

Cost to the school – $300.

To cover costs, we would need to sell 600 × 50p, and to make a $250 profit we would need to sell 500 × 50p, so 1,100.

19 A

0.7 × 300,000 – 0.3 × 50,000

= $195,000

PAPER C03 : FUNDAMENTALS OF BUSINESS MATHEMATICS

20 D

A pie chart is a circle.

21 C

A	$\dfrac{x^3}{-x^2} = -x^{(3-2)} = x$	correct
B	$(3a^2b) \times (-a^3b^2c) = -3a^5b^3c$	correct
C	$(1-x)(x+3) = x + 3 - x^2 - 3x = -x^2 - 2x + 3$	incorrect
D	$3x^2 + 6x - 7x^2 = -4x^2 + 6x$	correct

22 B

$1000 \times 1.03 \times 1.035 \times 1.032 = 1100.16$.

23 B

There are 360° in a circle, so if wages represent 60°, that is $\dfrac{1}{6}$ of total cost:

$\dfrac{1}{6} \times \$720{,}000 = \$120{,}000$

24 D

The mean is affected by extreme values, e.g. if nine people earn $100 per week, and one person earns $1,100, that makes the mean wage $200 when 90% of the sample earn half of the mean.

25 B

Coefficient of variation

$= \dfrac{\text{standard deviation} \times 100}{\text{arithmetic mean}}$

so $\dfrac{120}{3.6} = 33.33$

ANSWERS TO MOCK ASSESSMENT 2 : SECTION 8

26 C

x	x^2
3	9
5	25
7	49
8	64
9	81
11	121

$\Sigma x = 43 \quad \Sigma x^2 = 349$

$$\Pi = \sqrt{\frac{349}{6} - \left(\frac{43}{6}\right)^2}$$

$= \sqrt{58.16 - 51.36} = \sqrt{6.8} = 2.6$

27 C

From the normal distribution table, 20% of a distribution table lies between the mean and 0.53 standard deviation above the mean:

so $\quad x = 150 + (0.53 \times 20)$

$\quad\quad\quad = 160.6$

28 B

If 7% of the population is above 120, then $0.5 - 0.07 = 0.43$.

so $\quad z = 1.48$

$\quad 1.48v = 120 - 100$

$v = \dfrac{20}{1.48} = 13.51.$

29 A

$z = \dfrac{19{,}000 - 15{,}000}{2{,}000} = 2$

From normal distribution table:

$z = 0.4772$

So probability $>z = 0.5 - 0.4772$

$\quad\quad\quad\quad\quad\quad\quad = 0.0228$

$\quad\quad\quad\quad\quad\quad\quad = 2\%$

30 B

$$z = \frac{12{,}000 - 15{,}000}{2{,}000} = 1.5$$

From normal distribution table:

z = 0.4332

So probability z < 12,000 = 0.5 − 0.4332

= 0.0668

= 6.7%

31 B

Area between 12,000 and 19,000:

= 0.0228 + 0.0668 = 0.0896

= 9%

32 B

1,200 × 5.335 = 6,402

8 years annuity at 10%, from cumulative present value table = 5.335

NPV = 6,402 − 6,200 = 202.

33 A

495 = 250 + 25b

$$b = \frac{495 - 250}{25} = \frac{245}{25} = 9.8$$

34 A

35 D

Year 1	Depreciation	5,000
	Book value	15,000
Year 2	Depreciation	3,750
	Book value	11,250
Year 3	Depreciation	2,812.50
	Book value	8,437.50

36 C

$$\$8{,}000 \times \frac{1}{0.05}\,1 = \$160{,}000$$

ANSWERS TO MOCK ASSESSMENT 2 : SECTION 8

37 C

NPV = $1,000 (1 + 6.247)

See cumulative present value table:

= $1,000 × 7.247

= $7,247

38 B

Present value of 10 repayments of x at 7% = $100,000

From table $x = \dfrac{£100{,}000}{7.024}$

= 14,237.

39 B

This is a multiplicative model, so seasonal variations should sum to 4, with an average of 1 if there are four quarters.

If Y is seasonal variation for Quarter 4:

1.2 + 1.8 + 0.6 + Y = 4

Y = 4 – 3.6

Y = 0.4.

40 A

	Quarter 1	Quarter 2
Seasonal component	1.2	1.8
Actual sales	110,000	125,000
Trend	91,666	69,444

Trend has decreased between Quarter 1 and Quarter 2.

41 C

Working

Whilst Excel often does use the term you would expect in a function such as = NPV, at other times (such as with ROI) the word is less obvious.

42 D

Working

Excel can also find the MEDIAN and the MODE by substituting those words in the command.

PAPER C03 : FUNDAMENTALS OF BUSINESS MATHEMATICS

43 **B**

Working

A   Is wrong because without the brackets around the 1/6, the calculation would be 98 to the power 1, divided by 6

B   Is correct

C   Is wrong. This would calculate 1 divided by 6 to the power of 98

D   Is wrong. This would calculate 1/6 to the power of 98 (the same answer as C)

44 **C**

45 **D**

Working

The formula will alert the user if the two figures in cells D6 and D7 are not the same. If they are, the message will read 'OK', if not it will read 'error'. This may be used to check, for example, that the horizontal and vertical totals in a table are the same.